Life in Moscow
Communism and now

Axel Delwig

Life in Moscow
Communism and now

The book is a collection of short stories about what it was really like to live in Moscow, USSR in the mid-1980s. The focus is on different aspects of everyday life, such as shopping, reading books and newspapers, going to work, church, cinema, watching movies and TV etc, shedding light on some of the frequently bizarre problems we faced. This book is written from a first person perspective, with me being the main character. The first part of each story is narrated in a very personal and emotional style, and there are elements that can be sad, funny, ironic, optimistic or pessimistic. The conclusion of each story is written in a scientific style by way of an update of how matters have progressed in the last 25 years, i.e. up to the present time, to find a picture quite different from the official party line as well as common Western perception.

The book will appeal to the broad Western public with an interest in aspects of Russia and other Communist or developing countries; anyone wishing to travel, invest, do business or in any way be exposed to Russian reality (and in fact to the entire former Soviet bloc); as well as Russian expats interested in alternative interpretations of Russian reality. In addition, the book could also be of interest to readers in the post-Soviet space and the former Soviet Republics.

ISBN 978-1-62050-117-7

ID: 11462689
www.lulu.com

9 781620 501177

Life in Moscow;
Communism and now

Life in Moscow; Communism and now

Axel Delwig

Table of Contents

Preface

God, save Russia.

—*V. I. Dahl,*

My family and I lived in Moscow, Russia until September 1990. Since then we have lived in several European countries, but every year we return to Moscow to see our parents and friends. This allowed us to gain an interesting perspective on what has occurred in Russia over the years, since the fall of the Soviet Union. When we came back from Russia after each trip, our new friends would keep asking us what changes have taken place in Russia, if any. Thus witnessing this period of transformation in Russia's history, my family and I have collected many memories that I have now decided to publish as a book. This book describes what it was like for common people to live in Moscow in the mid-1980s in the ideology-driven, propaganda-soaked totalitarian society at the end of its life. Merriam-Webster defines totalitarianism as a political concept within which the citizen is completely subject to an absolute state authority.

The book also describes how I performed everyday chores: shopping; reading books and newspapers; going to work, church, the cinema; watching movies and TV; etc. It also sheds light on some of the frequently bizarre problems that my family and I faced. I try to end each anecdote with an update of how matters have progressed in the last twenty-five years, which leads the book concurrent to present day. The images of recent Russian history and contemporary Russian society that I hope to convey through my stories may differ from both the officially approved versions and common Western perceptions.

One can take nothing at face value in Russia—even life itself as a philosophical construct—neither during the mid-1980s nor in

2011. This book aims to demonstrate various layers of complexity within Russian society, and in order to do so, the stories and descriptions will start at the beginning of Soviet history, highlight the 1980s, and conclude with the present day. Several themes will be recurrent: the consistent make-up of people in power, the psychology of the Heroes of Eternal Marxism (THEM), the suggestion that Russia remains a communist country today, the anti-Russian platform of former Soviet Republics and Eastern European countries, and an alternative view of Russia.

The first topic of discussion addresses the particular make-up of people in power. After the Great October Socialist Revolution in 1917, the proletariat was unable to keep power. According to Marx and Engels, the proletariat is the most oppressed class in society and it was the proletariat that acted as the driving force of the communist revolution, which was a culmination of the class struggle between them and the bourgeoisie. The dogma maintains that after the revolution, the proletariat, together with all of the oppressed people in the world—a clause added by Lenin to form his own definition of Marxism—will govern by dictatorship and result in the destruction of capitalism, capitalist production, class division, and social inequality. Instead of being the driving force of the Revolution, the proletariat gave all and absolute power to a relatively small group of people: communist party apparatchiks, communist fanatics, the KGB and other power structures—otherwise known as THEM.

THEM and their progeny remained in power until the dissolution of the Soviet Union on 26 December 1991. A new generation of THEM, mainly from the Komsomol (Комсомол), which is an abbreviation for the Communist Union of the Youth, and an obligatory political organisation during 1918-1990 for young people between fourteen and twenty-eight years of age during the Soviet time. This new generation of THEM also came from the lower levels of the communist party, the military, and the KGB, and they came to power after 1991. Interestingly, most of the top political elite in Russia in 2010 were either born, or at some point worked close to the Mayor's office in Leningrad (currently St. Petersburg), on the brink of the 1980s and 90s. This fact is interesting from two different points of view: firstly the infamous October Revolution of 1917 occurred in St. Petersburg and secondly the Russian tsar Peter the Great initiated a revolution based on a westernisation of Russia in the eighteenth century, which he started by founding St. Petersburg and making it the capital of Russia. Therefore, the make-up of those in power in 1917, 1985, and 2011, remain the same. This relatively closed group of people has stopped at nothing to keep the status quo. THEM today live nearly in the same conditions as those described in this book; their appetite for cosmic-scale corruption, eagerness to accumulate wealth at any cost, extravagant taste, and flamboyant way of life are perpetual.

Many people today see Russia as a communist country, albeit with a slightly modified social and political structure. Its closest neighbours, the former Soviet Republics and Eastern European countries, still regard Russia as a dangerous and unpredictable neighbour. This book suggests a different viewpoint to challenge the consensual opinion regarding what is going on in Russia now. For example, I will offer a look at the Nord Stream Arbeitsgemeinschaft (AG), which is an offshore natural gas pipeline that will connect Vyborg, Russia, and Greifswald, Germany. It will pump around fifty-five billion cubic meters of natural gas per year. I will not go into details about the daunting environmental damage of the pipeline, the increasing dependence of Europe on Russian sourced gas, neither the political precedents nor the implications of the "arranging" rights to build this controversial pipeline from the neighbouring countries. Based on what I learned from the Nord Stream AG corporate website, the chairman of the Stakeholder Commission is Mr. Gerhard Schroeder, who is also the former Chancellor of Germany. Oddly enough, the website does not mention his Russian counterpart. The inauguration of the project took place when Mr. Putin was the Russian President, which leads me to make a reasonable guess with regards to the identity of the chairman's Russian counterpart.

I cover a variety of topics in this book. At times I may choose to address the reader directly; I may also answer questions that I would have otherwise heard in conversation. The use of these discursive techniques allows me to touch on disparate topics in a succinct manner. Everything written in this book is the truth as I have witnessed it. This is my testimony. Fortunately not everything described in these pages happened to me directly but it could have.

x

I have tried not to judge, as this is not my purpose. It took twenty-five years and huge effort to learn not to judge what I have witnessed, and I hope I have succeeded in removing such judgement from my testimony, albeit to a greater or lesser extent depending on the topic of discussion.

I would like to thank my family and my friends, Peter Calder, Shelley Lanser, and Anna Fialko. I would also like to express my deep gratitude to Lo Deufel, Elisabeth Warner, and Mrs. Brink for their helpful comments and suggestions.

How to Fix a TV Set

Television transmission is the particular type of mass media that serves the purpose of propaganda, upbringing, education, and organisation of spare time.

-Great Soviet Encyclopaedia

Our TV set was broken—not a big deal, one might think. However, it was immense big problem. What follows are the options that were available to someone living in Moscow circa 1985. First, we could have gotten a new TV. However, it would have cost at least three months' salary, without leaving money to eat and drink or to travel to and from work and therefore no opportunity to enjoy the most beautiful Metro in the world. The Moscow Metro, according to the myth actively advertised in the 1980s, was the most beautiful. However, the architects and participants of the Metro-Rail conference in 2008 voted the Warsaw Metro to be the most beautiful and the Stockholm Metro to be the most inventive. Regardless of the Metro sacrifice, there were few solutions to remedy our broken TV set.

Our second option would have been to repair the TV. This option was rather tricky because there were no viable services in the USSR. On one hand, the services existed, but on the other hand, they were just for show. This formality existed in soviet grocery stores as well. Food was often falsely labelled or incredibly expensive. Food labelled pork was often just lard. Most services in the USSR did not rely on customers (or customer satisfaction) to exist. Therefore, if you were to call a TV repair shop, an engineer who worked there would find no incentive to do the job, and if you were lucky, he may decide to actually pursue the work within a month's time. Although, a good bribe, would often accelerate the process.

Although many families in Moscow did not own a television, some great programs would air. Once a week there was a simplified version of a Discovery programme called *Club of*

Cinema Travellers. Actual travel of the USSR citizens was impossible, which explains the greatness of this programme. It featured a socialist country, not a capitalist one. No shops were visible because such images would disturb the people. During the show, the presenters would travel the sea by boat and those long 5 months of travel would be meticulously shown, as for example with Thor Heyerdahl's sea voyage with other 10 men, including Yuri Senkevich (USSR) on board of *The Tigris* reed boat in 1978. The show aired with plenty of commentary and very little visual stimulation. Once a month or so we would get the chance to see *Kinopanorama*, a movie review show presented by someone who actually saw movies by famous film directors. However, it did not seem fair to listen to discussions about movies that we would never be able to see ourselves.

Once a week there was programme called *In the World of Animals*, which showed ducks, rabbits, and occasionally more exotic species like dolphins. Again, there was plenty of commentary and the camera filmed the reporter from every possible angle but only occasionally did I have the good fortune of actually seeing a duck or a rabbit. The *Health TV* programme was another highlight within the world of television and it broadcasted useful medical advice. This show however became the context of a popular joke from my youth: a concerned mother in Irkutsk might ask, "From what age can one go out with a boy?" The reply went like this: "Well, one can go out with a boy starting from a very early age indeed, just make sure he is warmly dressed."

There was also the *New Year's Light* TV programme, which was the last possibility to see the familiar handful of singers performing patriotic songs and hear interviews with the "Heroes of Socialist Labour", i.e. prominent workers and peasants who showed extraordinary achievements at work. One example of an interview question might have been, "Please share with us your experience of how to outperform the day's plan by two hundred percent." A similar remark may have gone something like this: "This is all thanks to our Great Communist party, and in particular due to the personal contribution of the Great Communist Leader, Secretary General of the Politburo of the Central Committee of the Communist party of the Soviet Union, father of the nation, Leonid Ilyich Breshnev[1]!"

There were also old movies, which everyone would have seen numerous times, but the same old relics would air repeatedly. In particular, during the days of the celebration of the anniversary of the Great October Socialist Revolution, movies about Lenin's life would air endlessly. Each of these films exaggerated his overwhelming kindness, his extraordinary friendliness, and his care for children. However, Lenin's true influence was everywhere. He was the founder of the communist party of the Soviet Union and the follower of previous communist philosophers Marx and Engels. Lenin had developed the practical strategy of seizing and maintaining power in Russia from what had been only a theoretical existence of Marxism. Russia was a firing range from which this practical application of Marxist theory would expand to other countries and Lenin expressed this eternal vision when he famously said, "We came to power seriously and forever."

He also developed the theoretical and practical foundation for the suppressive communist regime. He justified genocide against Russian people: the wealthy, skilled farmers, people engaged in any intelligent or highly skilled work, nobility, aristocracy, writers, poets, etc. He endorsed the execution of the last Russian tsar Nicholas II and his family, laid the foundation for erecting the first concentration camps, and founded the Extraordinary Commission (Чрезвычайная комиссия, ЧК,) which predated the KGB (Committee of the State Security). Two of Lenin's devoted followers were Trotsky and Stalin who were contemporaries of one another. Trotsky developed and tried to implement the practice of a permanent revolution and Stalin promoted the principles of genocide and slavery, in particular among prisoners. According to estimates made by scientists and writers such as A. Solzhenitsyn, R. Medvedev, B. Ribakov, and D. Volkogonov, the number of victims of the communist regime in Russia ranges between twenty and one hundred and twenty million for the years 1921-1953.

Once a month, there was a programme called *An Evening of Laughter*. In spite of the bad title, the programme was actually good and popular. Although one might be inclined to wonder why, if the programme was so good, did it only air once a month? The accepted response would have been, "Well, why should people in the Soviet Union have a reason to laugh more frequently?"

There was an annual programme that one could see at midnight, whereas normally there was just a blank screen after this time. This particular programme aired only at Easter and featured foreign movies or foreign pop concerts, from socialist countries, of course. Thus it was understood to be an attempt to avert the people from going to church and participating in the religious ceremony of Easter, which according to the Russian Orthodox tradition takes place right after midnight. The question is – why would THEM want to avert people from going to church? This topic deserves a separate chapter, and I shall return to this question in "Let's go to church".

Did I miss out by not being able to go to church? I don't think so, not really, because half of the participants there would have been from the competent organs (THEM pretended that here was no KGB and referred to this organisation in this way) whose main task was to secretly photograph the crowd to use later for identification purposes. These competent organs represented at each place of work in the form of a special section within Human Resources would then have friendly chats with church attendees about philosophical and practical matters of life and death.

Young people like me just skipped this four hour long delirium waiting for the final thirty minutes dedicated to the *Melodies and Rhythms of Foreign Pop* programme from socialist countries and if we'd get lucky, we'd hear one song by a true Western pop group like ABBA at around 4:30 a.m. Many young people would be dead-tired and drunk by that time when they would suddenly see a light in the tunnel coming to the sounds of ABBA. This was a line of communication for us to other civilisation and it brought pure joy to the TV spectators. After ABBA wrote its famous *Super Trouper* song about a big circus drum, this pop group was forever placed on the black list. THEM decided to have a war in Afghanistan at that time and thought that this song contained a hidden criticism of that war, which was supposed to help the brotherly folk of Afghanistan. I wish they had asked us how we felt about helping our brotherly folk in Afghanistan, a war that cost us 30,000 casualties.

A group of actors from the *Theatre of Satire*, located in Moscow, created an extremely popular weekly programme with a name that loosely translates as *Bistro of thirteen chairs*. The programme aired from 1966 to 1980 and there were one hundred and thirty-three episodes. It was one of the first and most popular humorous Soviet sitcoms and it featured regular customers dining in a Polish restaurant. The original idea belonged to the actor A. Belyavsky who participated in a Polish serial *Czterej pancerni i pies* (*Four tank men and a dog*), which ran from 1966 to 1970.

Leonid Ilyich Brezhnev, who was the Secretary General of the communist party of the Soviet Union (and therefore the top politician in the USSR in 1964-1982) personally liked the programme, so the actors could do whatever they wanted for as long as he was alive. This programme provided Soviet people with the only possibility of enjoying current fashions within the relaxed atmosphere of a small bistro. The programme viewers could then observe normal expressions of daily life for individuals who were not frozen with ecstatic patriotism. The viewers could listen to informal conversations between others. They may even have heard a joke told between friends and they would have been able to listen to Polish music. The popularity of this sitcom was unprecedented. Women dressed and styled their hair just like some of the characters on the show (Pani Monika or Pani Teresa.) The actors became known in the public according to their roles on the show and the fans sent letters addressed to their character names (to Pan Professor.) People took photographs from the TV screen and then drew sketches of dresses and hats for reproduction. It was a true window to Europe for the people of Moscow.

I have summarised nearly ninety-five percent of the programmes that were available on the three to four TV channels that we had in those days, which gives you an idea of how little was available. The rest was the day's news and weekly political reviews simply exuded happiness towards the fate Westerners who suffered immensely from the uncertainty of tomorrow. The image of the rotten West that was displayed was that of a society paralysed by unemployment and strikes, deadly diseases, and natural disasters of all kinds on the other side of the Iron Curtain, which was a term used to describe the physical and ideological boundary that divided the USSR and other communist countries from the West after WWII, coined from Winston Churchill's Iron Curtain Speech on 5 March 1946. I remember vividly the happy and cheerful tone of the report about a fiery explosion of the space shuttle Challenger and the loss of its seven crewmembers in 1986. The newsreader was glowing with joy. The news and political programming often displayed the perspective that more and more people in the USA, Europe, and Africa were willing to support and join the communist parties in their countries. This gave the media hope that the West would thus one day cope with their deadly diseases, strikes, and natural disasters so that they could join the communist party. Ninety-five percent of the time one would encounter proud domestic reports (e.g. more cotton grown in the immeasurable fields of the republics of Middle Asia and more steel produced in giant factories) and thus the TV spectator could feel secure because THEM were designing and testing trans-continental rockets in the endless deserts of the country. These rockets would protect the country from the invaders that were waiting behind the Curtain. Yet, waiting there behind the curtain were the very same enemies who were reportedly dreaming of paradise in the Soviet Union.

Even with television being what it was, life was made bleaker without a TV set. Without a <u>TV</u> one might miss his or her monthly occasion for laughter or one might forget what a duck looked like. Without a TV one would be unable to see inside the shops. Or one might feel increasingly insecure because he or she missed the latest update on the rockets that protected the country so damn well.

My two-year-old son was reluctant to go to bed because he was expecting his favourite *Good Night Babies* programme that started at 8:15 p.m. This programme always showed some cartoon by the end of which my son would be sound asleep. I came to realise that I needed to repair my old heavy and bulky TV set, even though it had only four channels. It was then that I embraced the option of a TV repair for my two-year-old son. The question went like this: "My TV set is out of order. Is there any possibility for your engineer to come to repair it in the foreseeable future?" Granted I did not realise the naive context of the question that I was asking. It was 1984. I was just twenty-five years old and it was my first attempt at TV repair.

At first, there was absolute silence and then sincere and sparkling laughter at the other end of the line. Then someone tried to share this funny experience with his fellow comrades and the laughter became stronger, in the way that the thousands of participants of the Communist Party Congress would crescendo in their singing of the communist hymn *The International*. One would have thought that my question was the funniest thing this person had ever heard. I thought that I had made his day and that he would be telling this story to relatives and friends from then on after. Finally, he replied directly to me: "We are fully booked till the end of December, we do not have spare parts, we do not have ... be reasonable, man, tomorrow is November 7, no one will come today, we are celebrating already!"

That was it. It was November 7. Eureka! The peaceful demonstration of the Solidarity of the Working People and then the Parade of the Military Forces[2] would be showing a mere fraction of our mighty rockets!

I concentrated with earnest, I invoked Lenin's extraordinary kindness, and I feigned friendliness when I said slowly with a light touch of pity: "That is exactly my point. You see there will be the demonstration and the parade tomorrow. Are you saying that your company does not want me to share the enthusiasm of the people by celebrating the anniversary of our great revolution on TV? The next thing I knew, the engineer was in our room within ten minutes and repaired my TV set for free. This service was presented as a gift from the TV repair company to the customer of the year in honour of the anniversary of the Great October Socialist Revolution.

The reader may begin to wonder if it is worth repairing a TV set in Moscow in the present time. Post-Soviet television broadcasting propagates the idea that things can always get worse. Indeed when some had naively thought that TV in the Soviet days was dull and bleak, they were not prepared for what would come in twenty-five years. Today TV presenters themselves often speak in dialect and make frequent grammatical mistakes. This would have been unthinkable during the Soviet era. Today many Russian politicians also make similar mistakes with the Russian language, and when combined with the TV presenters, this may have been motivation for the reform of the Russian language, which was endorsed by the Ministry of Education and began on September 1, 2009. From then on if someone forgot whether the word for coffee was of the masculine or neuter grammatical gender, the new reform would discreetly allow both. In other words, the reform allowed individuals to write almost anything and it would be grammatically correct. It seems that the Russian language is being adjusted to a level more comfortable for THEM.

Television services went through excruciating phases of privatisation and deprivatisation. Believe it or not, these phases corresponded to the current comedy, spy, police, and prison shows. Many of the shows often featured a one-word title:

Officers	Marusja [a name]	Verdict
Escape	Efrosinya [a name]	Brigade
Voices	Admiral	Voronins
Apostle	Advocatesses	Wild
Gangs	Homeless	etc.
Snipers	Brothers	

The military and intelligence influence is evident and takes into account the military or KGB background of the people in power. Single word titles are easy to produce and understand. Two words need to agree grammatically, which can be daunting for Russian politicians. The appeal of these programmes is due to their titles and the content; indeed there is not much more interesting than prison breaks, violent interrogations, and pursuits of criminals. Therefore it is difficult to say whether or not it is worthwhile to repair a TV set today. However it may be said that the current TV line-up would most definitely benefit from a hint of diversification.

News programmes often consist of staged images of Prime Minister Putin in an array of military and civilian vehicles. He appears to be saying that in the event of a military loss, the chief of the military will at least be able to travel by plane, helicopter, submarine, or tank, that he knows how to throw a grenade and thus he will persevere.

The Russian President Mr. Medvedev is defending the intellectual front. Indeed, as in the Soviet days, everything is still a front, science, culture, agriculture public health, education. This simply means that extraordinary efforts and investments should be done to make things moving on. The President himself is supervising the construction of Skolkovo, a Russian equivalent of the Silicone valley, a town with an American touch of science and business. The former Moscow Mayor Luzhkov and his wife, as well as another Russian billionaire Mr. R. Abramovitch, own the state farm Matveevskoje, which is the location of Skolkovo, the proposed centre of excellence. Apart from the dubious location and land ownership rights, potential problems with recruiting and retention of employees, sluggish supply and infrastructure, funding, communications, and Soviet-like administration, the controversy surrounding this ideal city also centers on the fact that it will be run by the newly formed United Russians. United Russia (Единая Россия) is the main political party in Russia, chaired by Mr. Putin. Functionaries at all levels are members of the party. This means that state employees are decidedly in support of the party and thus the act of voting is rendered a simple formality. No official information on the number of party members is available.

On the bright side, there is a brilliant state-owned TV channel called Culture (Культура). It shows documentaries, talk shows, interviews, and shows of that nature on the subject of Russian and world culture. One of my favourite episodes was a tête-à-tête talk show called *Night flight* (Ночной Полёт) which ran from 1997 to 2009. In this show, the TV presenter Mr. A. Maximov would speak with the best actors, conductors, theatre and film directors, writers, poets, ballerinas, musicians, and composers of the highest calibre. Some of the guests on the show included M. Rostropovich (1927-2007) who was a famous Russian cellist, conductor, politician, and human rights activist who was considered one of the greatest cellists in the world and M. Plissezkaja (1925-) who was a famous Russian prima-ballerina and considered one of the greatest twentieth century ballet dancers in the world. The professionalism exhibited on set was the highest level possible, and it was painfully intelligent. Unfortunately the programme ended and one might speculate that it was the nature of its brilliance that caused it to end. Even though one might lament these limitations surrounding the scope of television in Russia today, one must not forget that just twenty-five years ago there was no television that was worth watching. I guess one could say that at the very least, things are moving in the right direction.

Are THEM Russians at All?

We are not shooting enough professors.

-V. Lenin

The title of this chapter alludes to the idea of what constitutes a good Russian. The title is provocative and slightly absurd. Typically, to be a good Russian is to be a patriot, that is to wish for the best for one's country, to act on behalf of the country's best interests, and to be able to use the Russian language adequately for communication. Thus patriotism was easy for THEM; however THEM's usage of the Russian language deserves some attention.

According to Cambridge Advanced Learner's Dictionary, a patriot is a person who loves their country and, if necessary, will fight for it. However, THEM appear to have their own definition of patriotic. Upon his dismissal from office, the former Moscow Mayor Mr Luzhkov was called a true patriot by Mr. B. Gryzlov, the Chairman of United Russia, the ruling party and the new political and business elite in Russia today. It was the former Moscow Mayor's wife who destroyed the architectural face of Moscow and amassed multi-billion US dollar wealth from the family construction business, speculative and illegal land schemes in Moscow and Moscow region, and money laundering. Another detestable action that exemplifies the absurdly patriotic vision of Russia today was committed local authorities when drunken teenagers burned a young man alive on an eternal flame memorializing the victims of WWII. This occurred in the town of Kolchugino in the Vladimir region just fifty meters from a local administration building. The local authorities, blindly in love with their country, tried to conceal the incident.

If upholding the Russian language is another example of patriotism, the subversion and deterioration of the language deserve some analysis. I remember being absolutely astonished when I failed to understand a shop assistant in a small rural village in the middle of the Ural Mountains, a mountain range that runs twenty-five hundred kilometers from north to south through western Russia, and forms the boundary between Europe and Asia. My encounter with this shop assistant was odd and particularly stands out in my memory because the Russian language is normally uniform throughout the country. This Uralian woman was describing an accident but she was using words and expressions that I did not know. I believe that she was speaking Feni. Feni is Russian jargon that is used primarily by prisoners. It was developed one hundred and fifty to two hundred years ago by street handlers to make their speech incomprehensible by others: in particular, gendarmes and policemen. The English equivalent of Feni is called thieves' cant. The original purpose of this language was lost during the Soviet period, as both inmates and guards spoke the language equally well. Feni must have then acquired a different context or it otherwise would have vanished. After the prison guards learned to speak Feni, it also became the language of THEM, as it was used equally well by both the guards and the former Russian President.

In one of his first press conferences, in Astan, Chechen Republic, on September 24, 1999, the President-to-be of the Russian Federation said, "We will soak (мочить) Chechens in the lavatory." Soak in Feni means to kill, that is to say that all Chechens will be killed in the lavatory. In *The Gulag Archipelago*, A. Solzhenitsyn described that to execute prisoners, THEM used gunshots through special holes in the walls of bathrooms and lavatories. Based upon the previous statement by the president-to-be, one can presume that Chechens were first imprisoned and then shot dead. This would take place, not in front of a firing squad, but in bathrooms and lavatories.

KGB agents and communist party members were often recruited from the working class and from peasantry. These people were heavily exposed to the Feni language of former inmates that returned to live in the same rural areas after serving their sentences because they were prevented from living elsewhere. They were not accustomed to using proper, standard Russian language, which would have sounded alien, grotesque, and suspicious to THEM.

The Russian language is complicated. It has been developing over many centuries, and when one speaks Russian, he or she may intentionally sometimes use certain words that Russian shares with Slavic or Old Russian languages to emphasise the loftiness or nobleness of a particular thought or situation. For example, there is the common word glazá (глаза), which means eyes and derives from Old Russian. Another word for eyes is ochi (очи) from the Old Church Slavonic and is associated with poetry.

If you wanted to refer to eyes with disdain, almost like a swearword of moderate strength, for example, if someone was staring at you in an impolite way, you could use the word zenki (зенки), which belongs to common folk's vocabulary and can be a great insult. However the word maintains its association with the common language. In a prison context, this word is substituted with morgali (моргалы), which in Feni can be associated with the act of blinking. This idea that one word can have multiple meanings and interpretations applies to nearly all words in Russian. Accordingly there are at least four distinct hierarchical levels of Russian language corresponding to the particular society strata, level of education, lifestyle, and even appearance. The word ochi is used by Russian aristocrats, poets, priests, and people in love. It is only with such a word that one would be able to describe the eyes of a beloved. The word glaza is used by most people while the word zenki is used in closed communities among like individuals, where it will not offend the other person. Although it may be used in particular situations to moderately and expressly offend the person to whom one is talking. Most Russians avoid the word morgali unless one belongs to THEM. I think that another reason why Feni survived is because inmates wanted to show complicity with the guards. The first and the last levels in the hierarchy of Russian language are so far apart that one may consider them different languages. This is why I believe that the shop assistant in that Ural village was speaking Feni, which I do not understand.

There is still another level of language called mat (мат), which is based exclusively on swearwords of highly offensive and rude connotations. Interestingly and counter-intuitively, the traditional folk who speak zenki are replacing it with mat, but not yet Feni. Finally there is the language sometimes spoken by young children who use words like guli-guli, or its synonym trua-a, which mean to go for a walk. In the early 1980s, glaza was strictly enforced as the standard language. At that time they still had two vitally important organs, the communist party and the KGB. However, with the demise of the former, most important, organ in 1991, the Russian language dropped to the Feni level particularly in urban areas. In the new millennium, you can actually hear more Feni spoken by politicians, on TV, in crosswords, and on the streets.

In order to demonstrate how THEM would understand less of a higher level of Russian language, consider the real street name Communist Cul-de-sac, which I noticed in the small town of Koselsk. This street name may be interpreted to mean that a communist regime is just a dead end. The mere existence of this and similar signs means that THEM do not appreciate this subtleness in our apparently common language, or else there would have been repercussions for such a diversion. I cannot accept that THEM has overlooked this blatancy considering the totalitarian nature of the regime.

Circa 1985 the intelligentsia developed and used a highly complex language in order to distance themselves from THEM and to serve as a form of linguistic opposition. The intelligentsia (интеллигенция) is a class of people who engaged in complex mental and highly creative work that sought to disseminate culture: writers, academics, teachers, etc. V. Zhukovsky, the founder of the Romantic movement in Russian literature, likely coined the term in 1836. The general public aspiration to acquire high language, such as the language used by the intelligentsia, may have had its roots in the popularity of highly sophisticated Russian poets of the late nineteenth to early twentieth century even though it was on the blacklist:

Afanasy Fet (1820-1892) was famous in the late nineteenth century. Fet's poetry exerted an immense effect on Russian symbolism, which was later exemplified by Innokenty Annensky and Alexander Blok in the early twentieth century.

Osip Mandelstam (1891-1938) was executed in Gulag, which is the second river point near the city of Vladivostok. He was one of the greatest symbolist poets of the twentieth century, a translator, and a literary critic. He wrote a famous Stalin epigram where he showed the horrendous famine that resulted from the Stalinist policy of collectivisation. After serving his first sentence in a Gulag, Mandelstam wrote several odes to Stalin, but he was arrested again during the most extensive cleansing of 1937-1938, sent back to the Gulag, and then executed.

Marina Tsvetaeva (1892-1941) was one of the greatest and most popular poets in Russia. Tsvetaeva lived and worked with her family in Europe in 1922-1939. Soon after her return to Russia, her entire family was executed and publication of her work was banned. She committed suicide on 31 August 1941.

Andrej Bely (1880-1924) was one of the leading symbolist poets, writers, critic. As a writer, Bely is known for his symbolist novel *Petersburg* (1916), which explores the hysteria and melodramatics of the First Russian Revolution of 1905.

Valery Bryusov (1873-1924) was one of the founders of Russian symbolism, a poet, a writer, a literary critic, a playwright, and a translator. Unlike many other symbolists, Bryusov stayed in Russia after the Revolution of 1917 and supported the new regime.

Boris Pasternak (1890-1960) was an extremely popular Russian poet, a laureate of the Nobel Prize in Literature (1958) for his novel *Doctor Zhivago* (Доктор Живаго, 1957) which depicts the private life of two lovers against the hurricane of the Russian Revolution in 1917.

Anna Akhmatova (1899-1966) was one of the most famous and acclaimed Russian poetesses. A significant part of her work was devoted to the intellectual and artistic exploration of Stalinist terror, repressions, and genocide. She was not arrested, but her husband, the famous Russian poet N. Gumilev, was executed and her son Lev Gumilev (famous Russian historian, ethnologist and anthropologist, who suggested revolutionary ideas on the genesis and evolution of nations), spent most of his life in Gulag, where incidentally he wrote a history of Russia using exclusively Feni language.

Nikolay Gumilev (1886-1921) was executed near the town of Kronstadt, Petersburg and was founder of the ACMEISM (from the Greek acme, meaning the best age of man, which strives to express poet's feelings directly through images movement in poetry). His unique poetry gives the reader a strong feeling of being present in the centre of a brilliant holy universe.

Based on the argument that THEM failed adequately use the Russian language I would argue that THEM are actually not

Russians. THEM do not fit into traditional definition of patriotism presented in this text. I contend that THEM are non-Russian usurpers similar to those who conquered Russia during the Tatar Yoke, which was a Mongol conquest of Russian territory in 1243-1480, and which established the dominance of Mongol-Tatar khans through their representatives (baskacs). Russian princes of the many Russian principalities had to pay tribute to the Khan of the Golden Horde. Due to the Tatar Yoke, Russia had developed the so-called east-west divide—a two hundred year delay in introducing social, political, and economical reforms, as well as scientific innovations, when compared with Western Europe. This Tatar rule also introduced the concept of oriental despotism into Russia and fits with the simplification reform of the Russian language, which lowered the level of the political language to Feni, and increased the tolerance for grammatically incorrect Russian.

This hypothesis also fits the state policy developed by Lenin regarding the genocide of the Russian people in the twentieth century. Lenin must have realised that genocide was an effective method of lowering the level of the Russian language and culture in general by eliminating native speakers. From the same standpoint, one may begin to suspect the assassination of Vlad Listyev on 1 March 1995. He was thirty-eight years old, a brilliant journalist, and the chief of the independent Russian TV channel ORT (now government-controlled Channel One.) Listyev's career in journalism was associated with the Perestroika, which was a package of economic reforms introduced in 1987 by Mikhail Gorbachev. Gorbachev was the Secretary General of the communist party of the Soviet Union from 1985-1991. The Perestroika aimed at boosting the country's stagnant economy in the late 1980s. This package included setting up self-financing state enterprises, which were virtually free of the former central control from the State Committee for Planning (GosPlan). The Perestroika also removed the need for permission of private ownership of business, eliminated state monopoly over foreign trade, and revoked the need for permission of foreign investment through joint ventures. This course was supported by Glasnost (which advocates the elimination of censorship), the democratisation of communist society, and the demilitarisation and strong peace initiatives, such as the withdrawal of Russian troops from Afghanistan.

Listeyv was also guilty of promoting the democratisation of the Russian society. This remains a life-threatening occupation in Russia to this day. Incidentally, Listyev would converse in a very good Russian language too. He was assassinated.

The Soviet Movie Making Machine

Of all the arts, for us cinema is the most important.

- V. Lenin

Movies sell illusions. Considering the extreme type of society that Lenin and company were building in Russia, THEM needed the power of movies to create the associated image, and thus illusion, for the people of Russia. There are several cult movies that correspond to three time periods of emigration from the Soviet Union and exemplify this type of image creation. In the first wave of the 1920s, roughly three and a half to four million people emigrated, which included people from the highest ranks of society: aristocrats, nobles, scientists, politicians, landowners, intellectuals, and other citizens who were loyal to the Russian Empire. The hallmark of this wave was the forced emigration of distinguished Russian philosophers to Constantinople on a famous philosopher's ship in 1922. The second wave of the 1940s and 50s, roughly eight to ten million people, left Russia during and after the Second World War and after Stalin's death. During the third wave of the 1960s and 1980s, about one million people left, mostly artists and members of the creative intelligentsia emigrated. This group had turned into dissidents as a result of their deep disappointment with the broken promises of the Khrushchev thaw, which took place between 1953 and 1964. The hallmark of this wave was the forceful emigration of the Nobel prize winning author A. Solzhenitsyn in 1974. This method of analyzing the three marked periods of immigration, as well as the role of Stalin, are important in being able to understand and predict the tendencies of the Russian movie scene.

Joseph V. Stalin (1878-1953) seized absolute power in 1922 and remained at the top of the communist party of the Soviet Union until his death in 1953. During this time, Stalin managed to build an airtight totalitarian society. He developed and implemented programmes of industrialisation, collectivisation, deportation of ethnic groups, the Ukrainian famine, the Purges, ethnic cleansing, pre-war and post-war Gulag concentration camps, well-organised political campaigns against wealthy farm-owners (kulak), scientists, doctors, Jews, religion of any kind, and culture. Estimates of the number of Stalin's direct victims range between twenty and one hundred and twenty million. The entire country was treated as a political instrument and a hostage that Stalin meticulously prepared, at any cost, to be the driving force of the world revolution.

Stalin considered cinematography as a pivotal ideological weapon and he, personally, controlled the production of movies in the Soviet Union. Accordingly film directors happily obliged to create films that contained an extremely high concentration of illusions in 1930-1950. For example, the movie *Bright path* (Светлый путь, 1940) pictured an uneducated pretty countrywoman, played by L. Orlova, who came to Moscow to work as a housemaid. Understandably bored sick with this job, she decided to work at the spinning mill, and within seconds, she was propelled to the highest ranks of the Soviet power structure. Having seen this film, I will never forget her fanatic eyes, frantic fixation for the spinning machines, and her final march along the line of spinning machines at the end of the film. To heighten the appearance of her jubilation for the viewer, there was the inclusion of her singing, "The march of enthusiasts:" There are no barriers for us at sea or on land, we are not terrified by ice or clouds. The flames of our soul, the banner of our country, we carry through worlds and centuries!"

Another such film, *Chapaev* (Чапаев, 1934), illustrates those defending the new communist regime during the Russian Civil War in 1918-1922. It began after the Great October Socialist Revolution in 1917 between communist supporters who were called Reds after the colour of blood and Russian Empire loyalists who were called Whites after the colour of bones. During this war about twenty million Russian people lost their lives and a further three million were imprisoned in Poland. In the film Vasily I. Chapaev was an uneducated red field commander fighting white generals loyal to the Russian Empire who had been trained in Military Academies. Obviously, during the entire film, Chapaev just kept winning battles against stupid white generals, and then he was betrayed and shot dead. After seeing this film, the euphoric bloodthirsty eyes of his machine-gunner femme fatale, Anka, as they are depicted during one of the battles have haunted me ever since. Interestingly Chapaev's name came to be used frequently as the target in Russian anecdotes.

There is also the cult movie Cossacks from Kuban (Кубанские казаки, 1949) that falls into this category of films but not because of the particularly engaging plot. The famous Cossack feasts depicted in this film serve as an illusion for the hopelessly hungry Soviet population that there will be an abundance of food sometime in the future. Ironically, the food shown in the movie was a fake. The common theme of the Stalin movies was ecstasy and unquestioning fanaticism in defence of building the new communist society, though sometimes I wonder if it could be stated that THEM started to fall under the spell of these illusions.

The next wave of movies released during the Khrushchev thaw was different because a new spirit of a free nation was born after Stalin's death, and THEM could not feed the audience with the same nectar anymore. The actors did not even need to act as much because the joy and elation from the newly acquired freedom was obvious in their eyes and body language. The Khrushchev thaw (1953-1964) was characterised by a moderate release of tight restrictions, sensory practice, and totalitarian control of cultural life in the Soviet Union. It was also the pursuit of a peaceful coexistence concept in foreign affairs, instead of a World Revolution idea. This time of Khrushchev's rule as the Secretary General of the communist party of the Soviet Union was necessary to detract attention and move the fault for genocide and other immense crimes committed by the communist party to Stalin personally. The release of millions of political Gulag prisoners, including Solzhenitsyn, resulted in a growing dissident movement on both sides of the Iron Curtain, revolts and unrests, including the Polish and Hungarian anti-communist revolutions in 1956, the coup against Khrushchev by the conservative Stalinist communist elite in 1957, and the replacement of Khrushchev by Leonid Brezhnev in 1964.

If any movies from the beginning of the Soviet period were worth watching at all, then I would recommend those produced in the 1960s. Many movies showed open, kind and friendly relations between people that was not based on fanaticism and fear of being reported to the KGB. However, the Khrushchev thaw ended in 1962 after the Bulldozer Exhibition when the KGB ordered to bulldoze an unofficial art exhibition in the Moscow suburban district Belyayevo. As F. Schiller had put it, 'Moor has done his duty, Moor can go now' This is a quote from F. Schiller's *Die Verschwörung des Fiesco zu Genua* (Fiesco, 1783) that refers to the delivery of the Moor to the enemy after he had done his duty – to arrange a revolt against Earl Fiesco's enemy tyrant Doria. This phrase became a saying that stresses the cynical attitude to a person whose services are no longer required.

I still enjoy watching those movies, such as about a noble and intelligent car thief in the style of Robin Hood *Beware of the car*, (*Берегись автомобиля*, 1967) or a movie about an intelligent red film operator during the Russian civil war showing the pro-tsarist white movement for the first time with great sympathy ('There served two buddies', 'Служили два товарища', 1968). One film that I have watched nearly one hundred times is *There lives such a guy* (*Живет такой парень*, 1964), which rediscovered the Russian tradition, the rich and strong countryside for city dwellers, or the fantastically popular comedies of the film director Leonid Gaidai. Gaidai amassed approximately 0.6 billion viewers, which is about one and a half times more than Steven Spielberg's record. The movies released in the 1960s do not disappoint; it was a time of creativity, good taste, and finesse for filmmaking.

I cannot neglect the greatest hits of the domestic movie market in making multi-part TV movies in the late 1960s to early 70s. Was it because the social pressure was too high and THEM needed to release steam? Otherwise, I cannot imagine THEM being so stupid as to endorse the release of these first intelligent movies often engaging the leading actors, directors, camera operators, and composers of the time. If so, it may have been THEM's first visible weakness, the steam may have been building up too strong.

Whatever the reason, in 1973 the absolute hit TV mini-series was released called *Seventeen moments of spring* (*Семнадцать мгновений весны*). The movie consisted of twelve episodes showing the last days of Hitler Germany and was centred on a Russian military intelligence officer who worked undercover in the Nazi Security Service headquarters in Berlin. With the best actors starring, music written by a leading composer, and the best TV screening time chosen, it was like a bomb explosion. For the first time, Nazi officers were shown as people and not just brute animals, even as intelligent people and not as stupid puppets, and sometimes even as attractive personalities particularly in the case of the SS Brigadenführer (SS Brigade Commander), Walther Schellenberg. I recently saw a documentary that reported that after the release of this movie Schellenberg's family had sent a letter to the actor thanking him for conveying an attractive and truthful image of Walther Schellenberg.

Even earlier in 1969, there was another hit *Aide of His Excellency* (*Адъютант его превосходительства.*) It was about a Russian intelligence officer during the years of the Russian Civil War in 1919 in the headquarters of a white general V. Z. Maevski-May. When I watch this movie over and over again, I have a feeling that my soul is at rest. In the end when the main character, of course, had to sacrifice himself for the sake of the working class, even this was done as a quiet and noble personal choice, and was therefore accepted as something that one will never understand but will truly respect.

There have been some other quite interesting mini-series about the fate of Russian peasants after the October Revolution. *Eternal call* (*Вечный зов*) and *Shadows disappear at noon* (*Тени исчезают в полдень*) are the best in my opinion. These mini-series addressed complicated relations between people who had been living together for generations in airtight communities and had developed their own civilisation. The cleansing that special KGB troops practiced towards wealthy peasants and landowners (kulak), who were considered supporters of the old regime, was not shown, but the resulting degradation of the Russian village was very painfully depicted.

The subsequent situation with Soviet movies in the 1980s was faceless, emotionless, dull, and senseless like a piece of granite. In fact, the early 1980s is officially called the stagnation period and due to a combination of factors, it describes a time when neither my wife nor I can recall a single decent Russian movie that was released during this time. The main task of this period was to find existing problems (often tiny and insignificant) and portray them with the constructive optimism of the spirit of the proletarian internationalism. The task was immense and there were not many talented artists left after the third emigration wave that took place between 1960 and 1980.

Themes of patriotism, work, and war continued to be heavily exploited. These themes were often a revisit to old stereotypes, or an uncovering of more facets to these themes. In addition, we were allowed to watch satirical comedies, historic films (not about WWII for a change) and adventure movies. It was during this time that the first nude images were shown on the level of Raphael's Renaissance Madonnas. It is understood that every word, actor, and shot were censored by the communist committee of the Movie Studio, Committee for Cinematography, and by the Central Committee of the communist party of the Soviet Union.

The granite-eyed actors were playing adventurers, lovers, poets, but somehow one could call their bluff because their texts were endorsed by so many committees. Behind their stone coloured eyes, there was a feeling of wistfulness on the cusp. The granite-eye expression was heavily used in the WWII movies to stress the horrors of the war, and the stupidity and barbaric nature of the enemy. In these films, everyone would conveniently speak Russian, look Russian, and have the vocabulary of an *Evening News* reader.

However small and insignificant, the movie market was dwindling quickly, and a normal person would never guess why. The reason was that quite often various artists would defect to the West, which was traditionally considered the most severe act of treason in the Soviet Union. However, unlike in the 1950s and before that time, the family members of the defector were neither immediately shot dead nor imprisoned. In the 1980s, the families of defectors were left alive, although they would be left without a future. This means that they would be unable to get a University degree, to pursue a desired profession, to travel, to get involved in politics, or to make any public statements. The family of a defector may be able to work as a janitor or in a factory, which would ideally be situated as close as possible to radioactive uranium, and as far from Moscow as possible. If the family member happened to have a profession at the time, he or she would have been deprived of all degrees, put on a black list, and would be lucky to find a job cleaning public toilets afterwards.

The domestic movie market was in fact dwindling. Instead of killing the defecting actor's family, THEM would arrest all prior work of the defector. All his or her movies would be withdrawn from the market; any mention of this actor would be banned forever. Unfortunately, the actors who defected were actually talented. Therefore the diversity of good movies was declining rapidly through this unexpected channel. The only access that we had to world cinema was in the cinema, not on TV. The few foreign movies available in Moscow, circa 1985 were mainly French, French-Italian co-productions, Eastern European, and some extremely rare American Westerns, typified by *Mackenna's Gold* (1969). I watched a few movies at a venue called, 'A week of Norwegian movies', a reasonably popular format of showing movies in the 1980s. The higher the film rating was directly correlated to the distance from the USSR border and from communist ideology and to bigger queues and higher prices on the black market.

'A week of French movies', was another impossible event, unless you were prepared to spend an icy winter's night in a tent outside the box office, or chained to the box office because of the special way that these tickets were acquired and then re-sold at tenfold price on the black market. There would be a well organised mob (we called them push-away guys) in the early morning and just push away everybody in the queue. Then they would remove the corpses of the frozen people and those chained to the box office (a sad joke, sorry) and buy all the tickets. Nothing personal, they just did their job and someone else's business. I cannot imagine what would happen if there had ever been 'A week of American movies'. My sad joke would surely become a reality. THEM knew it too, and there never was one. However, every summer there was a Moscow Cinema Festival with quite expensive tickets that cost approximately one day's salary. One of my most unforgettable experiences was of *Robocop* (1987) and *Convoy* (1978).

To quench our appetite for foreign movies, there were small but privileged movie theatres—one of them was ironically called Illusion—that for some reason showed movies like *The Magnificent Seven* (1960) or The *Seven Samurai* (1954). A normal person without connections could not buy tickets to watch those movies because they were too popular. I believe these were the only places where you could watch other less popular films starring C. Chaplin, movies directed by Reiner Werner Fassbinder, and classic old American movies, such as *Singing In The Rain*, *Casablanca*, etc, and interestingly also the last intellectual and highly spiritual movies by Andrey Tarkowski. Tarkowski (1932-1986) was arguably one of the most intellectual Soviet film directors. His complicated movies, such as *The mirror* (*Зеркало*, 1975), *Stalker* (*Сталкер*, 1979) and *The sacrifice* (*Жертвоприношение*, 1985) explored life as reflections, dreams, and religious obligations. To get tickets was a very difficult, but not an entirely impossible, task. A couple of times, I was invited to attend the exclusive screening events and to watch something truly different, such as *The Godfather*. In Russian we have a saying: "Water always finds a hole," which means something like "Where there's a will, there's a way."

I should mention that all of the movies except for those that held the exclusive screening status were heavily and constantly censored, such that you could generally never be sure what the main thrust of the movie actually was. I will give you just one example of a French movie *Les Ripoux* (*My New Partner*, 1984). At the end of the movie, which I managed to see at the Illusion cinema, an imprisoned police inspector, played by Philippe Noiret, was released from prison only to find out that he had just been used by his partner, a cop played by Thierry Lhermitte and he lost his share of one million dollars which they stole from a mob. In contrast, in the full version that my friend watched at the exclusive screening, Philippe Noiret was actually picked up by Thierry Lhermitte to share the booty. The movie was in fact about true friendship and not about treason at all. I can not begin to mention all of the scenes that were removed due to nudity, politics, shops, supermarkets, strong language, violence, or pretty much anything that had to do with the real life. The castrated foreign movies were supposed to contribute to the perpetual illusion of the decadent rotten West with no real values. Although the third period had different goals than the periods preceding it, on the domestic movie front, the impression remained that nothing would ever change.

The classical cohort of THEM stayed in charge for seventy-four years from 1917-1991, that is from the communist revolution until the demise of the communist party and the dissolution of the

Soviet Union, and creating illusions through movies was just one of the weapons in this huge arsenal. The scope and scale of the communist legacy cannot be comprehended from any human standpoint. Therefore, I would like to refer to the meaning of the number seventy-four in Feng Shui[3] numerology, where it means 'certain death'. Well, who am I to argue with Feng Shui.

The modern Russian writer V. Pelevin defined the new reincarnated generation of THEM as Generation П where П referred to the first letter of a highly offensive mat swear-word. Pelevin (1962-) is a leading intellectual and philosophical Russian writer. He is known for his novels, *Chapaev and emptiness*, *OMON RA* and others that describe Soviet experiences and propaganda clichés from the October Revolution in 1917, and the Soviet Space Programme. This new patriotic generation of THEM has adopted the "Après nous le déluge" ("After us, the Deluge") credo of Louis XV, and this highly destructive attitude towards life, culture, and society is reflected in current movies. They have become black, brutal, violent, and pessimistic. They are dominated by military, intelligence, or other types of investigations and operations. The few comedies are hopeless and tasteless, heavily exploring the theme of fun in drinking, sex, and anti-social behaviour. Family dramas are rare, looking at every aspect of life through a single distorting lens of obtaining (not earning) money. When I am persuaded to watch another Russian movie, with some very rare exceptions, I usually feel nauseous.

What is likely to happen next on the movie front? The most persuasive answer lies in the statistics. In the summer of 2010 all Russian movies on the domestic market collected 91.2 million roubles (~ three million USD) in ticket sales (last year this number was 439.5 million roubles, ~ one hundred and fifty million USD). If the trend were to continue, the estimated ticket sales in 2011 would be 18.9 million roubles (~0.6 million USD) and so on, which would bring the movie business in Russia nearly to a standstill. Another explanation for the decline in the movie industry could be movie piracy worth about two hundred and sixty-six million USD per year, which places Russia comfortably tenth in the world (if you can believe official figures.) However, most piracy occurs with the sale of foreign movies.

The bottom line is that Russians do not want to watch Russian movies anymore. This may be due to the devaluation of the old illusions that THEM continue to sell to us. Russians seem to be tired of the endless pursuits of criminals escaping in various automotive vehicles. We are unsure of who the criminal is in those pursuits or more generally, in life around us. Instead, we wonder if there are any non-criminals left in the political elite. Life and movie reality become too close, such that movie reality has no illusions left. It seems that the bubble of the Soviet movie making machine has burst and what we see today is a fountain of dim and sparkling fragments, which will condense one day to produce something completely novel, or maybe it will just fly around in vast emptiness forever.

Let Us Go to Church

Today in Solovki, tomorrow all over Russia!

-Solovetsky Camp of Special Designation

During hard times, people tend to seek consolation in religion, and life in Moscow in 1985 was far from extravagant. However, in the Soviet Union, Russians did not turn to religion in large numbers. Religion remained a prerogative only available to old and retired people who had nothing to lose. In the 1980s, it was an unquestionable and absolute fact that under no circumstances was one to go to church. No one knew exactly what would have happened if he or she did go to church, but no one went. This was a common trick that THEM would never inform the people because in their eyes, ignorance would make the people more afraid of the consequences of their actions. As a rule, one could never be sure that anything he or she did was lawful.

There had been rumours that if you went to the Easter church service, for example, THEM would photograph you, identify you and target your dossier. THEM were very serious and meticulous about everything THEM did. Even if you went to church looking for a life-threatening adventure, I would not recommend going as far as the confession stand, as most priests were recruited by the KGB as informants or were actually undercover KGB officers. The appointment of new clergy had to go through strict KGB endorsement procedures at all levels. Evgenij Tuchkov, the head of the sixth secret counter-religious department of the KGB between 1922 and1929, revealed that during that time alone, the official number of priests directly informing KGB increased from four hundred to twenty-five hundred in Russia. According to Gleb Yakunin[4], the collaboration between the Moscow Patriarchate and KGB was active in 1992, and there is no reason to think that the days of productive collaboration between the two KGB departments are over.

Of course, there was and there still is a well-hidden underground or so-called catacomb Orthodox church, which had separated from the official church after Metropolitan Sergij Nishegorodsky signed the Declaration of Cooperation with the Anti-Christ Soviet regime in 1927 resulting in the profound schism of the Orthodox Church into the official and the catacomb sections. As far as I know, no one has denounced this declaration to this date.

I did not know much about this at the time, but instinctively I felt two reservations about going to church and about official religious life in general: it was a dangerous activity for ordinary people and it did not fulfil its purpose even if you decided to be part of it. Akin to many other facets of life in the Soviet Union, religious life was a façade, pretence, a cynical hypocrisy, a shopping window decorated as if to serve its purpose, but in fact doing something entirely different. A lot of effort was made to undermine the Orthodox Church and religion in Russia in the first few years following the Revolution, because THEM regarded religion as the opium for the people. Therefore, the Soviet regime regarded religion similarly to drug trafficking, with all law enforcement apparatus, special and secret services, communist party organs, press, and media used to undermine its influence in society. By the mid-1980s, religion had no influence, the priests were either KGB informants or officers, and most churches were desecrated and used as military barracks, industrial buildings, warehouses, stalls, or public toilets. There was even the theory that official religion was a fishing hook to catch new prey for recruitment as potential informants. Some regarded it as a cover-up for sending KGB agents abroad or as propaganda displaying the conservation of traditional society structures in the Soviet Union.

It is understood that I could not buy or even *dostatj (get)* a Bible, baptise my child, or have a wedding or funeral service in a church. Just mentioning the name of Jesus Christ would have left me in a cloud of general suspicion, which might have led to a belief that I was crazy or leprous (i.e. I had nothing to lose.). Behaviours such as going to church could have been considered highly risky and designed to attract attention, to challenge the authorities, or to commit an act of covert dissidence.

This may or may not be true, but the common perception was that the KGB did not control churches further away from Moscow as tightly. Many people would travel far away from Moscow to baptise their children or themselves. So did I when I went for a baptising ceremony for myself and my two-year old son in an obscure church some three hundred kilometres from Moscow in the mid-1980s. It is possible that my personal KGB file still has a photograph of my happy face taken on that day. THEM destroyed the Orthodox religion was destroyed, and they gave the people a new communist religion in return. THEM killed Jesus Christ and the Orthodox religion for several reasons. The traditional and highly moral Orthodox religion would otherwise be successfully competing with the new immoral communist religion surrogate. The new religion also laid a powerful weapon into the hands of true communist believers and provided an absolution for all of their sins however transcendentally evil they could have been. The communist Bible is a brief course into the history of the VKP(b) by Stalin who provided simple answers to all possible questions, meaning that the new religion was simplifying people thus making THEM easier to control. In other words, the task was to downgrade the Russian people to the level of new political elite and to develop a new brainwashed Soviet person without much intellect, moral fibre, knowledge, hopes, and aspirations, something that the old religion could not provide THEM with, so their usual reflex was to get rid of it. Stalin used to say, "If there a man—there is problem, if there no man—there is no problem."

During the communist rule, Christianity was surgically removed and replaced with a rather primitive faith in a communist myth with all the necessary religious attributes, sacrifice, rituals, and bloodthirsty Gods. The core of the communist religion, propaganda, and ideology was the unquestionable faith in the new Gods, i.e. the General Secretaries of the communist party of the Soviet Union. Straight from birth, we had to swear allegiance to THEM in various forms from the Oath of the Young Pioneer for schoolchildren to various interviews probing our faith at work, in the Komsomol, in military service, etc. You could pass through the eye of this needle only with nothing less than diamond-strong communist faith or just with a boneless tongue saying the right things in the right place at the right time. I had chosen the second route, the downside being that it made me sick to my bones after a very short time.

In the 1980s, all streets in Moscow carried various slogans aiming probably at either enhancing or reducing our faith, such as the following not necessarily the most odious examples that immediately spring to mind:

Lenin lived, Lenin lives, and Lenin will always live! (Ленин жил, Ленин жив, Ленин будет жить!).

The victory of Communism is inevitable (Победа коммунизма неизбежна).

Communism is Soviet power plus the electricity for the entire country[5] (Коммунизм – это Советская власть плюс электрификация всей страны).

The party is wisdom, honour and conscience of the current era (Партия – это ум, честь и совесть нашей эпохи).

The slogans were growing bigger and bigger in size, but their influence on the people was getting progressively weaker. We just stopped caring about what was happening around us; we rejected their neo-Aztec cult and communist religion by common consent, and the communist regime fell apart like a giant with legs made of clay.

The Holy Patriarch Tikhon[6] who led the Russian Orthodox Church during its most difficult time after the Great October Socialist Revolution left three instructions upon his demise. The first one contained an anathema of the Bolshevik regime, the second urged all Russian people to be ready for immense suffering as a result of this regime, and the third commanded all true believers to spread all over the living world waiting for the establishment of freedom and proper order in Russia. This is exactly what I did as soon as I had the first inkling of a chance. We will await this "freedom and proper order" and return one day, but not quite yet.

A lot has changed during this time, new churches are everywhere, and the religious symbol of Russia, the Cathedral of Christ the Saviour, has been restored in Moscow. The President now attends the Easter ceremony on Good Friday, and you can see it on live TV. The political and business elite are reverentially placed in the vicinity of the Russian President according to tight ceremonial protocol.

The politicians have endowed the Russian Orthodox Church with huge personal and communal assets, land, influence, power, and independence. What did THEM get in return? Here is a citation from a speech of the new Patriarch of the Russian Orthodox Church Father Kirill[7]:

'The moral condition of society corresponds to the moral condition of authority. In accordance with the growth of morals and people's spirituality, those in authority will change accordingly. Russia should support Putin, the choice he made, as well as preserve him in power and strengthen his status'.

Compare this text with another statement from a Manifesto (presumably a pre-Presidential election statement) published by Mr. N. Mikhalkov 27/10/2010[8]:

'...we need to restore and to strengthen the moral authority of the people in power...we need to strengthen the vertical power of the authorities... we also need to adhere to our honour, duty and reverence for the rank of the authorities...'.

As a general observation and conclusion on the current situation in Moscow, more and more people from different layers of society have realised that it pays extremely well to be loyal to the politicians, powerful leaders and military or secret service, to feel and express reverence to all ranks of the authority, and that it is not a good idea to ask questions. Not that too many questions are left.

Newspapers and Magazines

The newspaper is not only a collective propagandist, but also a collective agitator and a collective organiser

- V. Lenin

I was not exactly a devoted and regular reader of too many newspapers in Moscow, 1985. As ninety-five percent of all TV time was generously devoted to all kinds of news, understandably I became a little fed up with news. TASS (Телеграфное Агентство Советского Союза *or* Telegraph Agency of the Soviet Union) accumulated, analysed, edited, and distributed all news. It was formed on July 10, 1925. The Agency collected and provided domestic and international information for newspapers, radio, and television in the Soviet Union. Officially, TASS belonged to the Cabinet of Ministers of the Soviet Union, but de facto it was a KBG news portal. It left no doubt as to who was in control of the game—the KGB. There was a joke that we used to say about TASS. Because the TASS headquarters was located across the road from the bookshop Progress, people would say that TASS is on the other side of progress.

However, it would have been a serious mistake to ignore newspapers in Moscow in 1985 altogether. There was a rule of thumb—you did not necessarily need to read them, but you had to subscribe to at least one or two. First, the everyday purpose of these newspapers could be inferred from a short sentence by Lenin himself who said of one particular communist-oriented piece of literature. He called it "A very timely book." A popular joke at the time stated that Lenin was in a toilet when he said this, but with the deficit of toilet paper at that time, it is hard to understand the truth of it. Second, THEM needed to know you subscribed, in a narrow and broad sense. Third, there were attentive neighbours and postal workers, who were keen to report things, as we used to say, where they were supposed to.

The newspaper Pravda[9] was at the core of the totalitarian structure and the communist party. Everyone had to have a subscription to this newspaper, even if you did not have enough money to buy bread for your children. Pravda was as essential for THEM as life itself. Many men died trying to get first Iskra and then Pravda across the border from Germany, England, or Switzerland into Russia before the October Revolution. Why bother? Lenin used to write a lot for these newspapers apparently giving practical tips on how to stir a Revolution and more importantly to brainwash the first communist fanatics.

Just like the communist party had its press organ, other Soviet political organisations also had theirs, such as Izvestia (Известия, News, organ of the Supreme Soviet Council), Trud (Труд, Work, organ of the All-Union Central Council of Trade Unions), Komsomolskaya Pravda (Комсомольская правда, Komsomol Truth, organ of the Central Committee of Komsomol, communist union of youth) etc. To show how trustworthy press media were in the Soviet Union, I would like to tell a popular joke about Pravda (Truth) and Izvestia (News). In Truth there is no news, and in News there is no truth!

Usually, in addition to the daily newspapers, communist and Soviet organisations would have their own monthly magazines. The propaganda, readership and the role of communist (Коммунист, monthly organ of the Central Committee of the communist party) can be exemplified just in one story about a red propagandist who came to an anti-communist white village during the Russian Civil War (1917-1922). During this propaganda session, the propagandist could have mentioned that all wealthy peasants (kulaks) were planned for extermination and deportation that all peasantry was considered to have anti-Soviet inclinations and therefore was targeted for extensive genocide. Maybe he also told them that very soon they were going to eat their own children during the infamous famine 1920-1921, and will have another chance to taste their flesh in 1932-1933[10]. We cannot really blame those villagers for what they did, as they quite rightly and predictably put the propagandist up on a stake, while he was still trying to convert them into the communist religion. The point of the story was not in the mercy of the Russian people, but in the perseverance in defending communist ideals to the last breath.

There were actually some newspapers, which were slightly more alternative and, therefore, much more interesting. First of all, I would like to mention a weekly newspaper called Literaturnaya Gazeta. This newspaper published intellectually rich articles, which often contained some well-hidden criticism of the regime, critical reviews on many subjects, including literature, cultural events, presentations, movies, and politics. The newspaper had its own style, image and status, it targeted the intellectual elite, and therefore it was allowed to be a bit Voltarian. It also had a very popular page sixteen (the last one) which was full of jokes, satiric poems, and funny stories. To my mind, Literaturnaya Gazeta was on the forefront of journalism at that time.

The weekly paper Agrumenty i Facty was supposed to supply some statistics about the Soviet Union, which had always been a state secret. So, the newspaper was in a bit of a corner, as whatever they disclosed was either treason or a lie. Unable to cope with the challenge of this fine balance, this newspaper fluctuated up and down.

I will use this opportunity to praise a popular science magazine Khimija i zhizn for those who wanted to read about science and beyond. They tried to keep up their banner in spite of all problems with finding qualified scientific writers, printing on low quality recycled paper and adopting an ancient design. This periodical probably was forced to publish special articles synchronising, for example, the lack of cherries and other fruit in the shops with evidence of the absence of vitamins there anyway. However, there was a breath of fresh air on its pages, I do not know how they did it, but they did their job very well.

There were, of course, many other magazines, such as ones about travel and ethnography (Vokrug sveta, Вокруг света, Around the world), about health (Zdorovje, Здоровье, Health) etc. I will also mention quite an odd publication called Krokodil (Крокодил, Crocodile), famous for its caricatures, which counter intuitively was not about animals, but dealt with a satirical representation of the Western lifestyle and some approved internal issues like alcoholism.

There were two magazines for women that I found: Sovetskaya zhenshina and Krestjanka, which were supposed to cover all possible secret desires a woman in the USSR might have (left). A real hit came, however, from Germany in 1987 in the form of Burda-Moden, which was extremely popular, mainly because it contained exact sewing templates of women's garments.

In any event, the goal of the press media was not to inform, but to modify the reality, to deliver the party approved attitude, way of thinking and conduct with respect to the particular events that occurred on either side of the Iron Curtain. For example, in 1958 the Russian writer Boris Pasternak received the Nobel Prize for Literature for his famous Doctor Zhivago. Immediately, Pravda (October 25, 1958) published an article by D. Zaslavsky called "The noise of reactionary propaganda about literary weeds" that called Pasternak an internal emigrant and set the tone for the subsequent persecution and victimisation of Pasternak. The official and non-official persecutors would normally say that they, of course, had not read Doctor Zhivago (because that would have been treason); but that they were convinced that it was an anti-communist piece of literature.

There were still some notable sparks of resistance though. I would like to tell you about just two children magazines: Murzilka and Vesyolije kartinki. Both were great. I remember reading the latter to my son or cutting out sequences of pictures to make a two-second-long cartoon. We made a decent collection of those cartoons, which we left behind. Those magazines contributed a lot to showing the total absurdity of the reigning stereotypes and underlying ideology. I will treasure the following poetry riddles in my heart:

1.

Look at that Bolshevik,

Who is climbing over there onto a tank?

He is wearing a plain kepi

He cannot roll his "R"s,

He has a bald head.

Guess who he is?

(The answer was LENIN)

2.

You chopped the whole birch tree into tiny pieces
With just one movement of your bare hands.
Who are you?
He answered quietly: LENIN!
And the people froze with wonder.

Judging from the modest circulation of the newspaper Pravda (currently just over one hundred thousand subscribers receiving three issues per week), there is dwindling demand for truth in Russia.

The Truth is gone. "The King is dead, long live the King." Whilst the communist party may be dead, United Russia—the not-so-different ruling party of today—lives on. Newspapers and other forms of media habitually look, feel, and sound as if they have been flattened by the steamroller that is United Russia. Indeed, it is hard to extract any reliable information from newspapers. One may read about eternal creatures buried deep in caves that come every millennium to boost the Russian gene pool. One may read about the Bermuda triangle, UFOs, extraterrestrials that operate in oceans, and other revelations of this kind. Certainly, Russian media is full of advertising, invitations to private Thai massages, and photos of Mr. Putin in various vehicles such as his driving extravaganzas on TV.

Russian mass media is faceless and toothless today. Mr. Ingo Mannteufel, the head of the radio station Deutsche Welle (German Wave) under Russian service in August 2010 claimed that there are no free mass media left in Russia. Granted, Mr. Mannteufel is not a Russian himself, and he may not know the bottomless depths of the mysterious Russian soul. But who does? Here is a quote by Mr. Alexander Dragunov, Editor-in-chief of the newspaper Yuzhnouralskaya Panorama, which receives funding from the government budget: "If it pays, work the way the authorities tell you to." It must be paying well.

Shopping for Things

We used to call the currency in the Soviet Union the *wooden rouble*. This is related to some shopping skills and a few tricks for buying or rather getting simple things in Moscow circa 1985. Forget the Western shopping experience in Russia, it is counter-productive. For starters, to buy something you should not go to the shops because you could not, with a few notable exceptions, buy anything useful in the shops. There are a few bits of travel advice for those who would venture to shop in Moscow 25 years ago, a city stuck in the time of the developed socialism. My advice would be, do not ask any questions in the shops. At the time, whatever one person needed, everyone else needed too. Therefore, these things were understandably not readily available in the shops, and hence should be acquired through other channels. This is the reason why Soviet people did not use the verb to buy. We used the verb dostatj (to get). Similarly, we would not describe something as being available in the shops, we would rather say something was vibrosheno, which means that it was thrown out on the counters, and by chance, it may, or may not be available in the shop at any given moment. This term can be explained as something useful that was delivered to the shop for a change, distributed mostly among important people and then the rest of the merchandise was allowed, or thrown out, to be sold freely. Important and good quality merchandise was thrown out very rarely, such that you would buy or rather get not what you needed or wanted at this moment, but what you would either need in the future or be able to exchange for something of equal value or for otherwise non-existent services.

A good simple example of what one might buy with a bit of luck and moderate effort in the shops was toilet paper. There was normally no toilet paper in the shops. You should never go to shops and ask about toilet paper availability. I am sure many spies failed just because of these unnecessary questions. To get the commodity you would need to observe people in the streets for a few days, maybe weeks, and I bet one day you would see happy women walking with toilet paper rolls arranged conspicuously in the form of ammunition belts across their chests. Our desperate spy should then follow the ant path of these happy women, and he would see a queue. This would be his initiation test. The password would not be, "What is being sold?" but instead, "Who is last in line?" The poor desperado should wait in this queue until he drops, struggles until the last bullet, is prepared to die there, and is willing to make it his last frontier. This is his destiny. If he does manage to get the toilet paper rolls, he should join with the happy women in wearing these around his chest.

A few examples of things that one may be able to buy in the shops without going to such elaborate schemes are low quality light bulbs, soap, and toothpaste. Depending on your life expectations, you could certainly buy habiliments of predominantly black and grey colours, very handy for funerals. All available shoes would leak, make you limp, make your stomach ache, make your self-esteem sink; any electrical equipment would fail to work or would need to be totally re-assembled. If you wanted anything to last, work, or function, then you would have to search for it. I just mentioned one way to track down certain merchandise. There were some others.

In reality, every item had its own channel of distribution, price, and value of human pride and self-worth, and social status. The best way to approach a shop assistant in a furniture shop was just to say the password, "twenty-five roubles on top," which meant a five days' salary. This would sound right and would attract his or her attention. That is exactly what I did when we needed some self-assembly furniture. You would need to offer approximately five percent of the price to the shop assistant as a sign of your gratitude. Bear in mind you could not assemble the self-assembly furniture unless you were a professional carpenter, desperate young man, or a lucky extraterrestrial life form with eight limbs. This self-assembly style furniture must have been designed in closed military bunkers without windows and therefore was good only as firewood. Not all fittings and holes matched, so you needed to make your own. The doors did not close or open depending on the particular exemplar and parts were missing. The colour of the delivered set often did not resemble what you had ordered.

Let's now talk about some things that could only be bought on the black market: jeans, discs of pop music, and ladies' boots. Buying books was another problem and I will cover that in a separate story. Each of the above items was undisputable luxury, which could propel you to the highest ranks of society, opening any door. Possessing those items was prestige in its most natural form. Almost invariably, these items would cost at least one month's salary. Therefore, you had to be sure you wanted to spend your entire month's pay on a pair of jeans. What should one do in this scenario? A good start would be to call your friends and say you were looking for someone who can get a pair of jeans not for you, but for one of your friends. This was not just a necessary safety precaution, but also it would send a signal that you had good friends and that you already had a pair of jeans. However, the problem was that there were a lot of people who were willing not to eat for a month to buy a pair of jeans, so you needed to be able to get something else in return, something that others were looking for, from car repair to chemical reagents for scientific research. People in Moscow during these blessed times called this type of activity krutitjsja, which meant to spin around. To spin around would be equivocal to busting your guts in order to get different things for different people in order to get other things from them in exchange.

Having said all that about Moscow in 1985, I honestly do not know what it was like to get things in the suburbs. Neither did the people who lived there. Therefore, they looked as if they were all going around with a bad stomach-ache to a funeral all the time. They would travel to Moscow from every corner of the vast Soviet Union every so often, and if they saw something, they would form queues like Egyptian pyramids or Stonehenge, forever massive and strong. These people from Kamchatka, or somewhere else, could survive lying in the snow overnight at thirty degrees below Celsius. Take my word for this you would not want to mess with them.

People called the currency in the USSR the wooden rouble because it was useless, just like many other things there. The role of this particular currency did not fit into the definition of a unit of exchange that would facilitate the transfer of goods or services, because there were no goods or services that THEM were willing to share with the people. Apparently, these days you can buy anything in Moscow.

The redistribution of what was previously bought and what remains creates an ongoing violent circle of merchandise. The gallery of examples is immense, and some of them are described in this book. Let us look at one of the conspicuous recent examples involving the story of a Mrs Baturina. This lady is the owner of the construction and building company "INTECO". According to Forbes magazine, she is the third richest woman in the world with a personal net worth of 2.9 billion USD just a bit behind Wu Yajun (The chief executive of real estate developer Longfor Properties, with a net worth of $3.9 billion) and Rosalia Mera (co-founder of Zara stores, net worth $3.5 billion). Mrs. Baturina is the powerful wife of the former Moscow Mayor Yuri Luzhkov. Just to name a few of her properties that can be identified using free Internet information - she owns at least three flats in Moscow (150, 150 and 445 sq. m), agricultural land of 2.85 hectares near Kursk), 35 hectares plot in western Moscow to build a golf club, a luxury hotel in the Black Sea resort town of Sochi, which will host the Olympics 2014 Sochi. Allegedly, she also owns a house Witanhurst (second largest privately owned house in London after the Buckingham Palace, a Georgian-style 90 room mansion with a ball hall of 3700 sq.m in Highgate, North London, worth $one hundred million) plus 50 million USD for a private cinema and 24-car garage, a luxury chalet in Kitzbuel, Hotel Grand Tirolia Golf & Ski Resort and villa in Vienna, Austria. She is apparently in the process of buying a castle in Carinthia (60 million euro), Austria. So, somehow, she has obtained exclusive development rights on thirteen hundred hectares of land (plus fifty-eight hectares to sell at will) in Moscow in 2007. She used this land for building penthouses and elite dwellings for Russian millionaires and thus changed the architectural image of Moscow forever. To build these new houses, about seven hundred historic architectural gems located in the centre of Moscow were reassessed as having neither architectural nor historical value and they were demolished. Visitors to Russia will never again see the Тёплые торговые ряды (warm retail rows), an architectural ensemble of trade buildings near Red Square designed by architect A Nikitin in 1864-69; some parts of the complex of the Cathedral of Elijah the Prophet built during the sixteenth and seventeenth centuries; parts of the reconstructed State Historical, Architectural, Art, and Landscape Museum-Reserve Tsarytsyno (Empress Elisabeth II, 1776); the Manor of Shahovsky-Glebov-Streshnevo, which belonged to Princess Shahovskaya-Glebova-Streshneva at the end of the 19th century; and too many others to list.

For undisclosed reasons, Russian President D. Medvedev sacked Moscow Mayor Y. Luzhkov on September 28, 2010. Usually something like that happens in Russia either because someone did not share enough, or that individual was preparing to do something really big. Was the Mayor going to acquire and subsequently sell the rest of Moscow or perhaps the Kremlin? Did it have anything to do with Skolkovo (the new town of excellence) that had been planned for construction on the land owned by Mayor's wife, which thus needed to be expropriated? The official story was that it was due to mistrust between the President and the Moscow Mayor.

In conclusion, the last twenty-five years have vastly increased the diversification and scale of the merchandise available for acquisition in the capital of Russia. For example, I have seen a news story about two mothers keen to sell their newborn children for about fifteen thousand roubles (five hundred USD). If this sounds too expensive, one can opt for the supersonic aircraft MIG-31 (NATO report name, Foxhound) that was developed to replace MIG-25 (NATO report name, Foxbat), six of which were sold by a Mr. Siljakov for one hundred and fifty-three roubles each (~five USD). If a clerk can sell a supersonic aircraft, what can people at the top sell? And to whom?

Currently Moscow offers the ultimate shopping experience to consumers, and if you want anything, it is only a question of money.

Shopping for Food

The present generation of the Soviet people shall live in communism!

From the 22nd communist party Congress, 1961 we all knew that we will live in communism at some point. Communism is a classless stateless society based on a common means of production. This is the ultimate political goal of social development, according to communist philosophers K. Marx, F. Engels and V. Lenin. The main economic concept of such a society is to receive contributions "from everyone according to their abilities" and give "according to their needs". The concept escaped my understanding until summer 2010 when I saw the Russian President Mr Medvedev paying in a supermarket for bread in front of TV cameras. His body language while he was holding the banknote suggested that he had not done this for a long time. The scene was similar to that in "My stepmother is an alien" (1988) when Kim Bassinger's character was paying in a supermarket and was asked whether she had smaller banknotes, after which she produced the same denomination note but of a reduced size!

According to the plans of the communist party of the Soviet Union, which were spelled out at the Twenty-second Congress in 1961, the Soviet people were supposed to live under communism from the year 1980. Evidently, my family and I belonged to the lucky next generation of the Soviet people who would be able to see what all of these immense sacrifices, victims, deportations, wars, genocides, and Gulag labour camps were about. Instead, what we witnessed were the final stages of agony in this foodless bleak society just before the Iron Curtain went down. The bottom line is that there was almost no food left in the stores. Maybe THEM ate all of the food in the Soviet Union.

One interesting observation from many foreigners in the early 1980s was that there were only very basic food products in the grocery stores, but surprisingly an abundance of food, delicacies, and various dishes on the dinner table on a special occasion. How was this possible? There were many facets to this problem revolving around the themes of where and how to get food and how to grow your own. Considering that you could not buy all the food items you needed, it would be a question of survival to learn how to preserve it in winter, how to eat on a daily basis, and how to arrange a party using all the food you managed to find, preserve, and prepare. There were ten indisputable facts concerning the food situation in Moscow in 1985, particularly during winters that would last up to half a year:

1. there was almost no edible food in the shops;
2. fresh meat or fish of any kind did not exist; everything was sold as frozen;
3. there was no fruit other than rotten apples;
4. the only vegetables available were potatoes, cabbage, carrots and beetroot; 50% would be rotten and would need to be thrown out right away upon purchase;
5. the bread was invariably stale, the sugar damp, and the milk frequently sour;
6. pre-processed food had no taste, and was unsafe for consumption;
7. safe food packaging was absent, carrier bags, wrappings for soft food like cheese or quark, and boxes for eggs were not available in the shops. People had to have paper, boxes, wrapping, and bags on the them all the time, as indeed it would be a shame to see eggs for instance and not be able to buy them as you did not have a box to put them in;
8. canned food was usually very close to the expiry date, as it was normally stored in special military storage depots for years before finally being released into the shops;
9. there were no spices except black pepper;
10. there were particular seasonal vegetables and fruits that were sold only during summer time, such as tomatoes, cucumbers, aubergines, grapes, melons, watermelons, and possibly a couple of others.

Now it was quite a challenge to buy food at the cheapest price and store it for the entirety of the long (in reality, very long, cold and dark) winters…

What food could you actually purchase for the average five to six roubles you earned for your hard day's work? A man's typical favourite shopping basket contained one bottle of vodka, plus one or two cans of fish in a tomato sauce, and some rye bread. The same daily salary could also afford you one of the following luxuries: 2 bottles of cheap wine, 1.5 kg of meat, or cheese, or sausages or butter, 15 litres of milk, 4 packs of leaf tea, about 5 kg of cheap fish or sugar, 50 kg of cheap rye bread or dirty potatoes which were never washed and were therefore half soil by weight, 5 dozen of the cheapest eggs or 3 dozen eggs of slightly better quality. I would say close to one hundred percent of an individual's wages would go towards the cost of food, notwithstanding a few days before the pay check being devoted to fasting. This situation has actually remained quite stable for pensioners. President Mr. Medvedev promised to adjust state pension to the level of the minimal official living standard.

One of the problems was that supermarkets did not exist, meaning that each food item was sold separately with the associated long queues. Some people tried to dodge the queues. It was popular to take a place in several queues simultaneously, constantly going back and forth from one end of a food store to another. In addition, you had to pay for whatever you wanted to buy first at a separate counter called a kassa. If you happened to buy things that were weighed, like cheese or butter, you would have to queue at the counter, so that the shop assistant would weigh them for you and then helpfully tell you the price for all the items individually, which you were supposed to remember; there were no pre-weighed food items available. The goods were then set aside and you would need to go back to the kassa to pay, waiting in another long queue of course. It was difficult to assess the quality of the food you were buying or enquire about the expiry date through the thick murky glass that separated you from whatever you were trying to buy. Really one was supposed to be happy with whatever he or she was getting. I like to think that this is why there are so many distinguished Russian philosophers.

Some basic food was available in the shops. Although I must mention the periodical nature of deficits that could randomly affect any product. For example, in 1984 all cheese products (two or three domestic types) disappeared from all grocery stores for quite a while. The next day, everyone knew how to prepare homemade cheese from milk that was still available in the shops. I still cannot explain where this information came from, as if the knowledge gene responsible for cheese-deficiency was suddenly activated in the entire population. Everyone was making reasonable mild cheeses at home and sharing recipes with colleagues at work, with other people in queues, in packed buses, trams, and on the Metro. Once I witnessed the following conversation between a police officer (militia man) and a motorist:

- *I see you like breaking the traffic code...*
- *I was just trying to deliver the best cheese recipe to my mother-in-law... I have some here, try it, sir!*
- *Wow, this is the best cheese I have ever tried. Just give me the cheese and the recipe and you can go for now, but do not break the law in the future! I will not always be as soft and tender as this cheese!*

A pack of Philadelphia-like soft cheese could have opened any door, bribe any policeman, you could get virtually anything you wanted from blue jeans to French perfume, even cut flowers, which women love so much.

Recognising the problem with the supply of food, THEM introduced so-called food orders which were distributed at work. These food hampers consisted of some essential and more rarely seen food stuffs, such as buckwheat, canned cod liver, canned oily fish, instant coffee, leaf tea, canned condensed milk, and better quality sausages and cheeses. The concrete list heavily depended on the hierarchy of your profession and place of work. For example, military and political organisations (Komsomol, trade unions, Soviet municipal committees) enjoyed subsidised canteens and superb food orders with everything one's heart could desire from champagne to caviar. I have heard of Kremlin hampers for current and former members of the Politburo – they could easily explain why THEM went to so much trouble to plot and execute the

Revolution and justify the regime during the following years of building Communism. Unlike all the rest of us, THEM had these hampers free and delivered conveniently to their doors. This reminds me of one joke performed by two comedians, V. Ilchenko and R. Karzev, about someone who was allowed just once to shop at their store.

-     *... Now I would like to get some fish.*
-     *Any particular type?*
-     *My God, I have forgotten what kind of fish varieties exist. Wait a second I will take, say, salmon.*
-     *How much?*
-     *Five kilograms.*
-     *The fish is fresh, it will not last. Are you sure, you want five kilograms?*
-     *No, I will buy six kilos and let this fish go bad...*

I will not dwell too much on growing your own vegetables and fruit, I had no dacha[11], and neither did my parents or parents-in-law. However, I saw the abundance of red-, white-, and black-currants, apples, plums, pears, cucumbers, marrows and so on, which the happy dacha owners would sometimes bring in to share with their fellow workers. In addition, how they could store all this treasure in tiny flats during those long, long, long winter times. I am not surprised that Lenin's body, as the Founder of the First (and hopefully last) Proletarian State and as the First Russian communist, (you will laugh, but his communist party registration number was indeed 00001) is still kept in the Mausoleum on the Red Square almost intact[12]. I would suggest that this was achieved because there were such vast skills in product conservation accumulated over these years in the Soviet Union. There is always a downside to everything though. We used to dry our own wild mushrooms, which we picked in the local forests, yet this spread a very strong smell all over the planet. After this pungent experience, my son still cannot eat mushrooms to this day.

So, what was it that we ate on a daily basis? I could re-formulate the question – What could we afford to eat?[13] Well, meat made a very rare appearance at the table, but potatoes and bread were the heads of everything, as they say in Russian, bread is the head of everything. Our family could only afford to offer meat to our young son, so we experimented for quite some time with soup made of cow bones sold for dogs in some shops, before coming up with the following gourmet recipe: two kg of cow bones and cook them with salt and black pepper for about two hours, add some animal fat, potatoes, and cabbage. Season it with fried onions and carrots. To make it special, you may add one to two salted cucumbers and dumplings. Beetroot was one of the nation's favourite root vegetables. We used to fry beetroot and then add it to the above soup (maybe with some meat and without dumplings) to get the famous Russian borscht. Beetroot was boiled, fried, pureed, and thus producing many interesting dishes and salads. People also grew some root vegetables, such as radishes, celery and horseradish.

There were many dishes made from quark (a kind of soft cheese) by adding some flour. These dishes had different names depending on whether the mixture was subsequently directly fried (syrniki; сырники) or boiled (lenivije vareniki; ленивые вареники), or alternatively wrapped in dough and then baked (vatrushki; ватрушки), fried (Georgian khachapuri; хачапури) or boiled (vareniki; вареники). In addition to this, obviously, cheap fish, sausages etc served with potatoes, rice or buckwheat were frequently on the menu. One could then recombine these ingredients for example, by adding quark to buckwheat or rice to processed cheese to make a salad. Cooking for guests was another story.

It was not unusual for a hostess to spend a few days preceding a dinner party almost entirely in preparation, such as baking sophisticated cakes, for example, a honey cake which required at least twenty-four hours to soften after baking before consumption. We had no money to buy vodka, therefore I used ethanol, which could not be bought in the shops–unfortunately I am unable to share with you where I got it from—to prepare homemade cherry liquor taking full advantage of the specialised shop Frosty (Морозко). For two days' salary, I used to buy about three kg of frozen cherries, which I squashed and mixed with ethanol, water, and a bit of sugar, the mixture would then be left to stand for about a month, after which it was filtered and bottled. The resulting cost was about one rouble per litre, which I could just about afford at that time.

Special attention was always devoted to salads. I used to prepare an array of ingenious salads at that time: eggs with rice, mayonnaise and canned salmon; processed cheese, with garlic and crème fraiche; cooked and grated beetroot with garlic, walnuts and mayonnaise; potato salad supplemented with eggs, sausages or ham, processed peas, salted cucumbers and apple seasoned with mayonnaise (Russian salad, Olivier); and very similar to the previous one but with salted cabbage and beetroot and without mayonnaise and sausages (called vinaigrette) seasoned with vinegar; and cod liver with potatoes and onions.

Green salad was out of the question, as peppers, cucumbers, lettuce and tomatoes were not available during winter. Salted herring, salted tomatoes and cucumbers were necessary on the table, as were salted or pickled wild mushrooms. Salami could also be seen on tables, although it was never sold in the food stores. After a quite long time to enjoy the starters with plenty of vodka or in my case cherry liqueur, there would be a break followed by a hot main course usually garnished with potatoes. Chicken was relatively expensive, so people did not tend to buy it, or if they did, it would be chopped into small pieces and fried with some spices, vegetables and gravy. Lamb was usually of a particularly bad quality because as it turned out it was bought by THEM (or some evil tongues say, it was just given as a gift) from New Zealand. This sounds normal except that this meat would come from sheep grown for wool and not for meat. Beef was twice as expensive as pork, so really the latter was the first choice for the meat stew with plenty of gravy. We used to have about twelve people in our eleven meters square room with Italian pop music playing all through the night. Add to this mayhem a cot with a two-year old son in the corner, three other neighbour families complaining about the noise. Believe me, it was great fun!!

Therefore, there was nothing in the grocery stores, but plenty of simple but delicious food on the table. It was a statement, a pose, a silent strike, a contraposition saying to THEM – we are still alive, we have our honour, we will survive, but perhaps *you* will not! Just before the end of their big communist experiment, there was nothing in the grocery shops left in the autumn of 1990. I am serious, there was no bread, no matches, and no soup; there was nothing left in the whole country at all. I thank God that we did not enter Communism, because what communist philosophers failed to convey was that passing the gate to communism was just like going through US Customs and Border Protection— no food allowed beyond this point.

By way of continuation of the above metaphor, food is now allowed in Moscow. However, in reasonably priced supermarkets and grocery stores, the food quality is very low and the prices are higher than in Europe. Domestic products are cheaper and less eagerly falsified than foreign food. Just a few years ago, you could buy decent fresh and frozen fish, but now it is almost impossible, so no fish in any form is highly recommended. The same thing happened to sausages and processed meat products. Most of their prices go beyond the affordability of most people and most products are invariably not fresh and often falsified, just like everything else from medicines to washing powder.

There are plenty of small supermarkets looking very much like their shabby relatives in provincial Greece and Spain, with about fifty percent of the space generously devoted to a multitude of vodka varieties and other alcoholic beverages. Vodka remains cheap, affordable and available twenty-four hours a day and seven days a week. The short phase of tasty bread is over; we are back to the same unforgettable and nostalgic smell of straw and dust in the bread section.

A solemn word of advice: never buy anything to eat from a street fast-food kiosk. In the best-case scenario, you will consume cat meat, dog meat, or human flesh. I have seen a TV report about three drunkards who killed, ate, and sold the rest of their companion to a street fast-food vendor. I would rather refrain from other comments on the taste, look, and consequences of a relaxing fast-food feast on a Moscow street corner. When I am in Moscow, I prefer not to eat at all, except for fruit, vegetables, and bread, loosing quite a bit of weight every time I go back...

Probably most people buy their fruit and vegetables at markets and bazaars of various sizes, which used to be everywhere, but are being reduced to just a handful. The buyer can judge the quality of a concrete product himself, which is important.

Falsifications are rare, but of course, you do not know whether these mushrooms, blackberries, or cranberries were not picked near Chernobyl. If you are able to close your eyes on this possibility, or if you have a Geiger counter[14] (many do have them), the quality and variability is usually excellent. In addition to fruit and veggies, these markets offer a variety of household items, tools, gardening supplies, plain garments and shoes, which are of domestic origin and are cheap, affordable and of reasonable quality.

The markets are the main place where Muscovites do their everyday shopping and buy food for conservation to consume over winters! This is enough reason for THEM to remove meticulously cheap markets from existence to replace them with shopping centres with where everything is at least double the price.

Shopping for Books

A book is the best gift for any occasion

I was over the moon. I just managed to buy from someone at work a spare copy of a brand-new Russian translation of *The Lord of the Rings* by J. R. R. Tolkien, which was published in Russia in 1983. I was going home by Metro squeezed tightly against two men who were also reading heavy books, and my heart was pounding with joy. I just could not believe my providence. It was once-in-a-lifetime fortune that I was in the right place at the right time to hear the music of the simple question: "Does anyone care for *The Lord of the Rings*? I have a spare copy." I was probably grinning like an idiot, as I noticed some undue attention to my persona at the Metro entrance, so I decided to have a look around and calm down. One fellow traveller pressed against the back door of the carriage was reading *The Forsyth Saga* by J. Galsworthy, which I absolutely adored and obviously so did this gentleman. The second Metro companion was going through the crime scene with the sleuth Sherlock Holmes by Sir A. Conan Doyle. There was nothing new for me to read over my shoulders, and I was just melting happily in anticipation of something exciting. My elated mood may sound a bit exaggerated, but let me explain something about buying, borrowing and reading books in Moscow in 1985, so that you can better understand my feelings at that time.

Buying or rather getting books was tricky business, unless you were keen to read all fifty-five volumes of the complete compilation of the works of Lenin or similar communist writers. If so, then you had tonnes of literature at your disposal. I have had my fair share of reading the required Lenin papers, and it was somehow not engaging me at all. I was always missing the point and could not picture the type of readership who would be interested in the stuff. It was too complicated for workers and peasants and too vague for intellectuals. He must have been writing for himself. Fine, we did not want to read this, in which case we could not read much at all. Buying anything was a problem, from a straightforward dictionary to a fiction book.

At this point, I should mention some interesting exceptions in the form of nineteenth century Russian classical literature, such as Dostoevsky, Chekhov, Tolstoy, Pushkin and other writers and poets less well known to the Western reader, some of whose texts were studied as part of the school curriculum[15]. Similarly, you could subscribe to works by quite a few European writers, such as Balzac, Zola, Hamsun, Feuchtwanger (but not his *Moscow-1937*, of course), just to name a few. The purchase of all these multi-volume subscriptions was arranged through a particular magazine called *Ogonyok (Little Light)* during the so-called *Khrushchev's thaw* in the early 1960s; however these books were not available in the shops in the early 1980s[16]. By that time, the bookshops were empty, just like all the other shops in fact. Apparently, we were supposed to buy works by Lenin as the best gift for any occasion, THEM wished!

To get a dictionary, a textbook or a piece of professional literature, you just needed to catch the time when once a year for a day or two specialised book shops like Progress would accept pre-orders, assuming, of course, that the dictionary you needed would be printed that year. Then all you had to do was just wait for a year to get a postcard that you could then proudly present in the shop and get your dictionary. You certainly could not phone the bookshop to find out when it would be available. You had to go everywhere in person, and must not forget your domestic passport. By way of an update, the situation with having domestic passports on you is still current. You still need it when you want to see a doctor, dentist, visit your friend at a hospital, buy a railway, or a plane ticket.

There was a possibility of buying old dictionaries in second-hand bookshops, and that was what I did when I needed an English-Russian dictionary. Luckily, there was such a shop close to our flat, and the one I finally bought after many attempts had been published in 1942!

On other occasions, I was not so lucky. There were no textbooks when I was going through higher education in the late 1970s and early 1980s. Indeed, why would someone need a textbook if there were plenty of Lenin's works in the shops? I was studying Biochemistry and wanted to buy the textbook *Biochemistry* by A. Lehninger, a Russian translation of which has just been published in the early 1980s. In any case, I called many times at the second-hand shop called Medical Store in the city centre. I made friends with the shop assistant – a nice lady in her 60s. During the first ten or so visits, I learned a lot about her life, I knew the names of everyone in her family, and when I was enquiring about the health of her grandchildren, I was referring to them by name. Well, we cannot always win, can we? On the bright side, I managed to get a brand new English-Russian dictionary just after two years of persistent hunting. Therefore, life is full of compensations, as W. S. Maugham elegantly put it.

There were not decent books in the library. Libraries were empty, completely and utterly useless. On the other hand, you would not seriously expect them to be filled with good and useful books, textbooks, dictionaries, if there were no such books in the shops? In science, this phenomenon is called a negative gradient; meaning that any matter, including books, will go in the direction of the gradient and even THEM cannot change the laws of physics. You could not find books you needed/wanted in a library, but you could borrow them from friends, and friends of friends, and friends of friends of friends. Most twentieth century literature I had read at that time was borrowed through this long-winded chain – E. M. Remarque, H. Hesse, H. Boell, A. I. Solzhenitsyn, V. V. Nabokov[17], A. P. Platonov[18], B. L. Pasternak … You had to read them quickly, within one or two nights, and then these tattered wonders would make their risky and noble way to some other lucky fellow who did not want to accept Lenin's works as a present.

I was part of the chain, too. In the 1980s, I was once in the German Democratic Republic (GDR) and bought a two-volume compilation of poetry by M. Tsvetaeva. I also got as a present an absolutely astonishing philosophical fantasy novel *Master and Margarita* by M. A. Bulgakov[19]. I still keep this book with nearly transparent and unreadable pages, which were once turned over by thousands of fingers and rubbed clean.

You could not buy any of the afore-mentioned literature through something called the book by post system, because there was no system. Basically, some readable books were published not only in Moscow, but also in other parts of the country where the Russian language was less popular. The publishers wanted to sell these books, and they would even send them out by post if you happened to know that for a change they might have published something more interesting than a *Short guide to the history of the Communist Party of the Soviet Union* by Stalin. There was no Internet at that time, of course, so the book could have been published by your neighbour and you would not have a clue. The only success worth mentioning was my acquisition of *Twelve Chairs* by I. Ilf and E. Petrov[20].

There was a bizarre idea behind a very popular route of book acquisition in the 1980s – in exchange for recycled paper. On the surface it might sound fine, you would just take twenty kg of paper for recycling (God knows how) to a small remote office, wait in the usual queue to keep you in form, just for a couple of hours, well, maybe three. However, in exchange you would get a voucher allowing you to buy a book, exemplified by 'The Woman in White' by Willkie Collins and later an endless historical series of Moris Druon[21]. One problem is that those books quickly became a kind of fetish of high social value. People would take to recycling booths secret documents, rare antiquary books, scientific journals.

Just for the sake of completeness, I will mention three more channels of book acquisition in Moscow that I used with varying degrees of success in the 1980s. The first of these was through a particular second-hand bookshop that I knew would always put any new acquisitions on display after the lunch break (2-3 pm). I would arrive 15 minutes before 3 pm to see a group of interested readers who had made similar observations about the fate of new acquisitions in this shop. The rat race would start at 3:00 pm and finish at 3.01 pm. Everyone behaved; we were not fighting for an ultra-rare salami sausage after all. In addition, not everyone could actually fight. I was always last even when I glued myself to the door like Spider-Man, so this way generally did not work for me very well.

The second way was to go to the Dzerzhinsky (he was the first KGB chief in the 1920s) Square dominated by the KGB headquarters… Strange idea, is it not? Not really. On Saturdays, in one of the three corners of this infamous square there was a black market of books, called 'Tolkuchka'[22]. Finally, once I found a very interesting book "Methods of interrogation" published by the KGB, which, I assure you, was very informative. I also found a less informative book, but a real marvel, the *Legend of Thyl Ulenspiegel and Lamme Goedzak* by C. De Coster, in a rubbish bin. I assume that someone must have just received a book as a gift and got so excited as to throw out another book of the same thickness to free some space on the bookshelf.

Their effort to prevent us from reading excellent books was extremely counterproductive, as this was the best advertising for the particular books one should actually read. Thanks to THEM, I had read many real masterpieces, which I probably would not have read otherwise. Through your network you could get almost any book you wanted, read it overnight and treasure it for the rest of your life. In the middle of the night, I would sometimes take a break from reading, look out of the window and spot the lights still on in a few other windows – someone else was reading, too!

There has been unquestionable progress in this area resulting in the abundance of books of all kinds in Moscow now-a-days! You name a book, and I will find it for you. The plethora of books ranges from previously banned dissidents and defectors, such as V. Suvorov[23] and A. Solzhenitsyn to popular books for children (something that was particularly difficult to buy in 1985)—really anything that your heart desires. The availability of books in foreign languages is less impressive, but nowadays people go abroad more often, such that buying a particular foreign book is not such a problem.

Books clearly became less dangerous to THEM. The common Western perception is that it reflects democratisation and freedom of expression... It could well be! However, I suggest we should conduct a little independent investigation into what is behind this vast planetarium of books in Moscow in the present days. Our small research project will not harm anybody! Here are the results of this study[24]:

Thirty-three percent of Russians do not read any books, and sixty-six percent of the people do not read fiction;

Books are too expensive [with an average salary of ten thousand roubles per month (three hundred and fifty US dollars) or even thirty roubles (1 US dollar) per month in the agricultural sector[25]], an average book costs two hundred roubles (six US dollars)], such that fifty percent of Russians in all age groups do not buy any books. According to the NarKomStat[26], in an average month Russian people spent 7.45 roubles (~0.25 US dollars) on books, CDs, DVDs or printed mass media including newspapers and magazines[27];

Children's reading is plummeting. Indeed, in the last seven to eight years children reduced their reading by thirty to forty percent. The reason seems to be the introduction of the pragmatic school curriculum that teaches children on a need-to-know basis;

Seventy-four percent of people after the age of fifty-five do not buy any books[28];

Pitiful budget of the local libraries resulting in an annual reduction of book collections by five to seven percent.

Illiteracy in Russia is growing at a rate of eight to ten percent per annum. Two million teenagers are illiterate, and the overall level of literacy ranks Russia as the one hundred and twentieth in the world together with Cameroon and Bangladesh[29].

There is something of the Pyrrhic victory[30] in the current proud parade of books in Moscow, taking into account that Russians are becoming too poor, old, illiterate, busy or just uninterested in buying and reading them.

End of One Archipelago

The knowledge of Gulag archipelago is vital to our society.

-Mr. V. Putin, Agency VESTI, 26/10/2010

It was spring 1983, and I was twenty-four years old. My jacket pocket was burning in spite of all my efforts not to attract the slightest attention to its content. My friend gave me *The Gulag Archipelago* by A. Solzhenitsyn[31], which was a serious criminal offence and would have qualified for a long imprisonment for me, my friend and of our families. Or perhaps just me, depending on whether or not lending me this book was merely a provocation. In the USSR, lending this particular book to anyone was an act of absolute trust, and borrowing such a book was such an act, too. Why would anyone do something like that? Why lend, why borrow? Because we wanted to know the truth, and this feeling is stronger than fear.

Once I asked my friend who actually gave me this book why his hair turned grey so early in his life. He told me the story behind this book. He bought it obviously abroad whilst at a conference. He spent all the money he was allowed to exchange on this book and it happened when the shop assistant was handing the book to him. An accompanying person from the so-called *competent organs*, i.e. the one who was *accompanying* the Russian delegation came into the bookshop and was rapidly heading towards my friend. Within mere seconds, my friend's hair turned grey, which distracted the attention of the *accompanying* person, while the shop assistant managed to replace the deadly book with a merry children's book.

With 'The Gulag Archipelago' in my pocket, the feeling of danger was so intense that I still remember every stone under my feet, which were dragging too slowly to a small filthy communal flat. The smallest room was occupied by my family, and it looked like we were going to occupy it for the rest of our lives, as you could not move house at will in Moscow, 1985. Never before and never since have I experienced this feeling of a novice on a minefield. The colours became brighter, sounds richer and stronger, time slowed, such that I was not sure whether this day was really over yet. EVERYONE was an enemy; it was enough for anyone just to whisper:

- *Look, he is drunk..., he looks unusual... he looks strange...he is wearing glasses...*

and I would be doomed forever. Try it, it is fun, but you cannot make a single wrong move, this is the only problem. Because if you do, you and all your loved ones will go with you to the Gulag – this is how it worked. No mercy from anyone, and I mean anyone. You are a soldier, you can only trust your partner, and only in combat, because he is covering your back, just like you are covering his. Therefore, personal relations were and still are stronger than steel.

I was reading the book behind closed curtains or in the lavatory and I thought that no one saw me with this book. The book was stored under a loose floorboard in a dirty and smelly plastic bag. I was naive and wanted to know the truth. After having read this book, I was not naive any more and I learned the truth about THEM. I will not comment on the book, after reading it the scar from the wound it made will remain forever and nothing will ever be as it was before. More pertinently, how was I to return it now? The book had been lying under the floor for quite a while already...

Someone must have seen me obviously. Not the pleasant old couple from the biggest room in our communal flat; they were nice pensioners and had their fair share of the Gulag and Nazi camp experience. Not the young family with a daughter, struggling to survive just like us. I suspected the alcoholic couple with three deranged children.

THEM came in at once and within milliseconds filled the entire four bedroom flat housing four families. I did not have enough time to sneeze and they were all over me like glue. I cannot remember whether the doorbell rang. Quite possibly, they were able to pass through walls like cockroaches or seep through the ceiling like poison. They did not wear masks for at least two reasons, first, because they looked all the same anyway and second, because they did their noble job. They knew what they were looking for, where it was and they wanted it ASAP. It was early November – the anniversary of the Great October Socialist Revolution – and they wanted to report another closed case of state treason. Therefore, they skipped the more traditional 'pre-heating' period of intensive interrogation, which also involved asking questions they knew the answers to.

Flashes of light, the screeching sound of broken old oak floorboards, the impatient hand searching for hidden treasures – how many times has this scene been repeated over and over again in human history? This time they did not find the book – it had been completely consumed by mice together with the cheese-infused plastic bag, and the hand surfaced full of mice droppings...

The alcoholic couple did not get their well-deserved reward in the form of our filthy room, which they wanted for their deranged children. They should not complain as one of their children survived after birth only because my wife had enough breast milk to feed two mouths.

The abridged edition of 'Gulag Archipelago' adopted for the school curriculum has been published in Russia in 2010. The irony of the citation is that it was state treason to read, publish, and distribute this book, strictly enforced in the USSR by the same people as the author of this citation. THEM welcome Solzhenitsyn's works with open arms in Moscow of today. Works of this author are part of the school curriculum, he is not dangerous anymore, probably because it was so long ago, and we all know that everything is so much different now.

However, there are some books banned from publication in Russia, because these books are obviously dangerous. To such category belongs a book by Mr. S. Belkowski[32] 'Putin's business'. I am sure blacklisting this particular book has nothing to do with the allegations published by German magazine Die Welt of twelve November 2007 in an article by Manfred von Quiring 'Warum Putin gar nicht Präsident bleiben will?' ('Why Putin does not want to remain President?') that Mr. Putin owns four and a half percent Gazprom[33] shares, thirty-seven percent SurgutNefteGaz[34] and fifty percent of the oil-trading company GunVor International BV[35]?

One thing is crystal-clear - this could not have anything to do with the imprisonment of Mr. Khodorkovsky and subsequent capture of YuKOS[36] oil business by GunVor International BV. Indeed, the man could be the richest person in the world (worth up to $70 bn, according to Mr. Belkowski).

Interestingly, the black list of books in the USSR included authors who wrote the truth about history, questioned philosophical concepts and showed the brutality of the regime. The current regime is apparently so much different that these books have only a historical interest, while other and more obvious concerns can mark a book as black now.

Learning a Foreign Language

The inclusion of the subject 'Foreign Language' in the curricula of secondary schools and higher education institutions serves an entirely ideological purpose, that of bringing up a communist person

-Explanatory note, Bogatova N. M., http://www.portal-slovo.ru/rus/pedagogics/207/3083/

I must confess that I failed to learn a foreign language at school, just like everyone else in Moscow, 1985. It was not that I was particularly lazy or extraordinarily stupid; it was because I was not really supposed to. I suppose that instead of a foreign language, THEM would rather that I learnt the communist Bible, 'Das Kapital' and 'The Communist Manifesto'[37], by heart. Well, maybe some of Lenin's works as well... I am personally convinced that by preventing us from learning a foreign language, THEM were freeing more space in our heads for those dusty communist principles, as well as erecting an 'internal' Iron Curtain within each person in the Soviet Union. I learned English with language courses after graduating from school, and it was the only way to do it at that time. As for this book, my son helped me with the language side of things.

A seemingly simple question – how to learn a foreign language? Like anything else in Moscow, 1985, it was very difficult indeed. I am not talking here about the apparent difficulty of spending the required time and effort to learn a foreign language, but about the logistics of this exercise. As I mentioned, it was very difficult, if not impossible, to learn a foreign language at school, unless it was a special elite language school[38], which were opened by way of an experiment first only in Moscow in 1963 and subsequently spread to other major cities in the Soviet Union. I think it has something to do with the Cuban Missile Crisis in 1962[39], which must have revealed amongst other things the lack of proper foreign language training in the military and general population in the USSR. For the sake of argument, maybe the whole crisis was some kind of a linguistic misunderstanding.

Let me continue. In these special schools the pupils would start learning a foreign language from age eight, as opposed to from age eleven in normal schools, with at least six lessons per week in the first few years increasing to eight to nine lessons towards the end of the curriculum. Firstly, there were not so many of these special schools in Moscow[40], and secondly, these schools were extremely competitive and therefore difficult to get into. In addition, even in these special schools the colloquial language was not taught, so eventually pupils could read, write and translate, but they could not master everyday basics. Another problem was the location, location, location of the schools and their catchment areas, and, finally, most of these special schools were offering German and a few of them English, with just a handful of schools offering other languages, such as French. My interpretation is that because Germany was considered as the most plausible enemy in a future war, we were supposed to know our enemy's language. The logic was as solid as a rock. After graduating from a normal non-elite school with just two foreign language lessons per week, pupils could hardly recognise the words of this language. It is understood that they could not speak or read at all.

What if you wanted to learn, say, English after, by default, you missed the opportunity to learn it at school? Certainly, you could become a professional in this area, and in this case you could apply for a five-year English degree at various institutes, such as the Institute of Foreign Languages (Maurice Thorez Institute), Moscow State Institute of International Relations, Moscow State University or Faculty of Foreign Languages at the Pedagogical Institute. One catch though, you could only pass the tough entry exams if you were educated at a special elite school.

Otherwise, you would have to resort to a sparse network of language courses. In the 1980s, there were just a handful of evening courses in the entire multi-million city, which were extremely difficult to find out anything about. The foundation level courses had a two-year curriculum with lessons from 6:00-8:30 pm three times a week. After these intensive and very tough courses, you would be able to read and speak at a very basic level. There were just two places in the whole of Moscow that offered one-year advanced level language courses. Finally, there was a single possibility to become a professional translator or interpreter by taking additional two-year evening courses at the Institute of Foreign Languages.

I went through the first two hoops of this sophisticated torture. Not everyone was that motivated, with about half of the students dropping out every half a year, such that after three years only about two percent of the original class survived, with just one hero out of roughly one hundred starters who might decide to go on to study for the translator diploma in English. The third year was particularly tough (see 'Going West'). I will forever treasure the memories and remain eternally grateful to three lady-teachers, three zealots, three devotees of the principle of adult foreign language teaching. If you ever read this book, thank you from all my heart! Because I left the country straight away. After those courses, you could read, write and speak at the normal European level. It was just like an operation on a blind eye, which was seeing only hazy images before and then became as sharp as a tack. There was a severe deficit of dictionaries, which was solvable. As far as books were concerned, there were several possibilities of buying English fiction books, like special foreign language book sections in some specialised large bookshops and second-hand stores specialising in foreign language books.

I remember one particular small second-hand foreign language bookshop that I came across on a tiny street in downtown Moscow. I was struck by an absolute silence inside, despite being packed with people. It was as if we all were members of some kind of prestigious cult with complex silent rituals that banned even page rustling. If you needed to communicate with a shop assistant, it was to be done in a dying whisper, and even then, you would almost certainly feel that you were on the brink of breaking some long-standing and honourable tradition. By being capable of reading those books on the shelves, we seemed to have acquired some eternal knowledge. Maybe it was just a shared respect for our achievement and endeavour in learning a foreign language. I remember an elegant ritual scene from the movie *A Beautiful Mind* (2001, starring Russell Crowe) about a Nobel laureate, the economist J. F. Nash, when the professors of Princeton University were silently surrendering their fountain pens to Nash in recognition of his achievements.

There was also a further catch if you knew a foreign language. A very rare few with good command of a foreign language would be treated by others with envy and suspicion. Perhaps diplomats and teachers of foreign languages would be excluded from the general aura of suspicion, as they were supposed to be professionals in this area. Nonetheless, those with good foreign language skills would be treated by normal people as possible spies, dissidents, potentially dangerous and politically unreliable rotten intelligentsia. Even in the 1980s, normal people would instinctively ask themselves (and some of them not only themselves) – how did he/she come to speak a foreign language so well? And why? The logic was that there was no system to learn it, so he/she must have learnt it there (as we say 'behind the hillock', 'за бугром', i.e. behind the Iron Curtain), so he/she must be a spy!

I have talked to some people who had learnt English after school like myself, and it transpired that we did this partially because it was a challenge, "a foreign language resistance movement" if you will, a statement that we dared to wish something more from life than THEM could offer. Historically, the English language was associated in Russia with aristocracy, tradition and honour, all being extremely rare commodities in Moscow, and we wanted to be part of that. In any case, I did complete eventually the English course. During that time, I was completely engrossed in learning grammar and vocabulary list twenty-four hours a day and seven days a week, on the metro, on the bus, at work, before, during and after sleep. I kept a vocabulary book under my pillow, I was writing all words I am using now on my hands, face, and wallpaper, everywhere. Slow and steady wins the race! If you take into account my absolute lack of memory, I reckon I did pretty well. By learning English I have done what I had always wanted – I have destroyed my internal Iron Curtain!

Today, in Moscow English courses are everywhere, you are free to learn this beautiful language, no problem! Prepare your wallet though, a decent course will set you back at least 80,000 roubles (eight months' average salary) for an intensive eight-months cycle, similar to the one I did in Moscow, 1985 (I paid fifty roubles, i.e. less than a half month's salary, which is more than a sixteen fold increase in price).

Clearly, not everyone can afford this surge in prices, but maybe the schools finally free from KGB supervision now provide solid teaching of a foreign language, similar to that in German and Dutch schools? Here is the opinion of an ordinary school language teacher on this matter[41]: *'This is a very sad topic. Having many years of working in an ordinary secondary school, I have to admit that in most cases the school teaches a foreign language not so much as a subject, but merely tells our pupils about its existence'*.

On the bright side, people on the streets of Moscow today, particularly young people are quite likely to understand and be able to answer your question in English. Certainly, special private schools, colleges, private tutors, courses at work teach languages, but these channels are affordable only to the elite. However, even the elite sometimes fails to use language when necessary, as judged from a meeting between the Russian President Mr. D. Medvedev, American business executives and California Governor Mr. A. Schwarzenegger October 11, 2010. One of the few young Russian students who obviously was carefully selected for this purpose failed to finish a single sentence in English and switched to Russian.

In conclusion, it would seem that the level of foreign language teaching at school, as well as the cost, quality, availability and affordability of courses in adult further education, still remain inadequate in Moscow of today.

Everyday Marxism-Leninism

Marxism-Leninism and proletarian internationalism

Marxism-Leninism philosophy was the official ideological platform of the Soviet Union. It postulates the leading role of the communist party in social development towards the ultimate goal – communism. Unlike the classical Marxist dogma of a global revolution leading to the establishment of communism all over the world, Leninism considers the possibility of achieving this ultimate goal in just one particular country. Proletarian internationalism is a key concept in Marxism-Leninism that makes the proletariat the main driving force behind the entire movement towards communism. Proletarian internationalism also denies patriotism, as the ultimate goal is the same for the proletariat all over the world. According to this concept, the new United Russian patriots, such as the former Moscow Mayor Mr. Luzhkov are classical proletarian internationalists.

I was probably about five or six years old. I remember lying in bed in kindergarten for the traditional Russian midday siesta looking sleeplessly at the portrait of an unknown unpleasant bald man with a beard. He did not look like a pirate and even less like Robinson Crusoe because his name was, according to the label, Lenin. I reckoned that this could not be possibly a proper name for a proper pirate. What was his portrait doing between our colour pencil drawings and a picture of a hedgehog? Who was he?

In the first grade of primary school, I learned a few things about that mysterious person who, unfortunately, was not a pirate after all. First, we were told that he liked children very much, which I doubted because he always looked very strict having a severe look about him. Secondly, apparently, he devoted his entire life to making everyone happy, but he did not look happy at all. How could it be that someone who was trying to make all people happy was never happy himself? Really, it would have been easier for everyone if he just turned out to be an unusual-looking pirate.

Then very soon, I became a Little Octobrist[42] and got a badge in the form of a red star with a portrait of the omnipresent Lenin, this time as a child. The child was trying to smile, but this feeble attempt did not look convincing enough to me. Do not think that becoming a Little Octobrist was easy. To become eligible, I needed to prepare a poster about a great communist or event. This poster in A0 size format was called Stengazeta (Стенгазета), and it was supposed to be displayed on the wall to teach us a lesson. I did not know a better topic than about V. I. Lenin, who was the best fighter ever for us Little Octobrists, and when he had spare time he also fought for workers and peasants. I had learned quite a lot from this poster of mine, but it seemed that the more I knew about Lenin the less I understood about him, as he did not look like a fighter at all. Moreover, I was not sure why Lenin decided specifically to fight for workers and peasants, and for instance, not for florists' assistants (I liked flowers). First, these strong men could fight for themselves, just as I did with various degrees of success when someone at school would bully me. Second, if worst came to worst, this feeble looking person could not possibly have been much help to them in his old shabby suit jacket anyway. Somehow, I felt that I was supposed to understand all this nonsense, so I started pretending that I did. Basically, whenever someone asked you about Lenin at that time, you were just supposed to tell this person the above information and you would be just fine.

I had some temporary problems in upgrading from being a Little Octobrist to a Young Pioneer, I cannot remember why. Was I too shy, too plump, or too skinny? Did I not collect enough recycling paper to be eligible? Who knows, God works in mysterious ways... For a short while, I envied Young Pioneers because they wore Pioneer red ties, and they were considered mature enough not to be constantly reminded of Lenin, so they could discontinue wearing the badge with 'Lenin as a child' portrait. At that time, I liked the history of ancient Rome, Greece and then the Middle Ages, so I nearly forgot about the poor devil.

In my Komsomol period, I heard the name of Lenin many times every day. There was nothing more to learn about him as a person, except that he had a family, two brothers, three sisters, and a wife and was very hard working and talented for his age... Instead, we would spend hours and hours reading his works and articulating what they were all about. It was impossible, nobody in the class could make any sense of the stuff, with notable exceptions being that Lenin seemed to be cross with many people, such as a bloke called Kautsky[43], a woman called Zetkin[44] etc. Everyone in the class was put on the spot to answer the teacher's questions almost every day, and it was pure torture. Until one day... I was hiding behind the tall desk trying to turn into a fly, an ant or at least a mouse. "I see you are hiding your knowledge about the key concepts of communism, Axel. Would you be so kind as to share your vision with us?" I heard our history teacher's voice.

Instead of turning into a mouse, I turned into a hypocritical nightingale – I was singing like a bird. Since that time, it was never a problem for me to talk about Lenin's ideology, philosophy, any implications of Marxism-Leninism for building the first communist state, women's rights, the class struggle, rotten bourgeois economics and politics, and favourite communist dogmas about merging cities with villages, intellectual and manual work and all classes in society. At the peak of my abilities, I could talk for the entire lesson to save others. You are free to disbelieve me, it sounds implausible, but this actually happened to me in real life, it was like magic! I just stopped thinking altogether. Instead of trying to understand, I tried not to and instead turned everything upside down in my head. In this game, good was bad, black was white and so on. By that time, I had read and acquired Marxist phraseology, which is really a separate language altogether, and then just like with Lego, you assemble and dissemble a few concepts of this ideology in a bit of a random fashion, and voilà!

I remember doing the same tricks at University and then later when I was taking exams for getting a PhD, which were called PhD minima[45]. I had been working further on this new talent of mine. I was not only able to talk, but also to ask tricky questions, ones that would engage the teacher in a long proliferative speech. Sometimes I would enter into a passionate argument, a scientific discussion, an intense polemic—THEM loved these chess moves of mine. The key aim was to undermine the faith of the teacher, and then he would spend a lot of time defending it. It was real fun to me because as we say in Russia my tongue has not got any bones, and neither had my faith. I was just singing and saving others.

This was nearly twenty years ago. I cannot sing these songs anymore. When I see the same portrait of an unusual-looking pirate, I feel sadness with a bit of bitterness. Who was he really? A German spy? A meagre intellectual who hated his country, his people and his culture? Someone who just tried all his life to avenge his brother's death[46]? An advanced syphilis sufferer with a deranged mind and degraded body? A merciless tyrant? And importantly, what was his portrait doing in the kindergarten between children's drawings and a picture of a hedgehog?

When I was going through the scientific communism course for the PhD minimum, I heard the following joke:

- *What is philosophy?*
- *Philosophy is similar to looking for a cat in a dark room.*
- *And what is Marxism-Leninism philosophy?*
- *Marxism-Leninism philosophy is like looking for a cat in a dark room, whilst knowing very well that THERE IS NO CAT THERE AT ALL!.*

There is nothing to argue about, to dispute, to struggle for, to remember, to teach, to be taught or even to contemplate. There is nothing to nurture, to protect, and to believe in with the whole Marxism-Leninism philosophy because there is no cat there at all!

The communist era in Moscow is over, but more people who belong to THEM continue to live under communism, i.e. giving to society some of their work or sometimes giving nothing at all, but taking whatever they want in return. This situation urgently requires some kind of an underlying philosophical interpretation, but the paid philosophers cannot oblige with any reasonable theory of why should it be tolerated. Marxism, Leninism, Stalinism did their job well in saying that this is necessary for the subsequent victory of communism all over the world.

The Russian Church and intellectuals (as exemplified in Mr. Mikhalkov's Manifesto that I alluded to in Let's go to church) came up with an idea that the answer could be in the strengthening respect for the authorities and people in power on the basis of Russian nationalism, traditions, old Orthodox and family values. Whilst I can understand the benefits of adapting the St. Paul's Civil Obedience doctrine[47] to the needs of a modern communist state I must be missing the logic of strengthening obedience to the authorities, which are mostly corrupt, criminal, extremely inefficient, illiterate and non-patriotic in the usual sense of the word.

With this in mind, we can take an educated guess as to the type of society being built in Russia, as those portraits of Lenin between children's drawings and a picture of a hedgehog are now eagerly being replaced with portraits of Putin and Medvedev!

Getting a Flat

Currently there are 147,000 families registered for municipal flats in Moscow. New apartments are currently being allocated to families which were registered in 1988-1990.

-Odinzovo INFO, 22/04/2008, http://www.odintsovo.info/news/?id=21993

The property market in Moscow in the 1980s consisted predominantly of municipal flats (traditional communal flats for several families to share, or the more modern type for an individual family), with a small fraction of 'cooperative' flats, i.e. built for private purchase by wealthy people with good connections and society status. In particular, the 'cooperative flat' system welcomed with open arms those belonging to the Soviet nomenclature of different levels, such as those working in large industrial plants, public servants of all kinds, obviously members of the KGB and the military, diplomats and other people with foreign currency. 'Cooperative' flats were built by Ministries, Academies, the communist party and secret service organs.

In the early 1980s, my wife and I lived in a microscopic municipal communal flat in Moscow occupying the smallest room of eleven m^2 (118 sq. ft.). We could not afford a so-called 'cooperative flat' because it was too expensive, in particular for a young family (i.e. it would be equivalent to ten years' salary) and almost impossible to get into this system. We could not be registered for a new municipal flat either, as the minimal qualifying quota was five m^2 (54 sq. ft.) per person at that time, so, ironically, we had 1 m^2 (eleven sq. ft.) too much from the generous Soviet point of view. The registration for a municipal flat was a bit of pretence anyway, as the queue was about twenty years long. In fact, we were lucky to have this lamentable room after all, as most of our friends went on living with their parents after marriage. So just like with everything else, THEM had no spare flats available to us, fine! Somehow, we were not surprised, and I suspect neither are you by now. I had heard of the possibility of renting a flat, but a month's rent would have been two months' salary. Therefore, after starving for a month, you would still be in debt by one month's salary anyway. Loans and mortgages did not exist at that time.

In 1982, our son was born, and it changed our life. For the purposes of this story though, I will continue looking through this particular prism of getting a new flat. From this standpoint, suddenly we appeared to have less than the generously allocated five m^2 per person, so I filled in the relevant forms, collected the necessary documents and registered for a new municipal flat with the opportunity to get one by the time my son had reached his twenties. The neighbouring young family (Katia, Victor and their child Olga) that occupied a slightly bigger room in the same flat and did not qualify for a separate flat even with a child did not want to wait so long. Katia was working unpaid as a clerk in the local municipal housing office, and after five years, she was supposed to get a new individual flat (and she actually got one.) She had no choice anyway, as she was not a Muscovite, and had no right to get on the 'property ladder' in Moscow at all. I should mention that living in Moscow was a privilege, and only people born there were entitled to do so. Obviously, there were and always will be exceptions to any rules, such as the 'brain drain' from other parts of Russia or indeed the other Soviet Republics[48].

The biggest room in our communal flat was occupied by a nice old couple in their 80s, and I guess they just never got the chance to see the end of the long queue for an individual municipal flat. Quite possibly, THEM have strict rules to do everything in their power to turn our lives into a living hell; therefore each communal flat had to have a sociopathic alcoholic couple. The particular alcoholic couple allocated to us had three deranged children. One child was a bit of a philosopher – he enjoyed spending hours in a dark storage cupboard, but the rest were incarnated bandits. Sometimes their father, when he was not busy drinking some very cheap and foul-smelling alcoholic beverage and beating his wife (often banging her head against the wall separating our rooms), could also be found in the pleasant darkness of the storage cupboard—his eccentric habits possibly originated from Diogenes of Sinope[49] himself. Certainly, he celebrated his eremitic loneliness by drinking cheap vodka and/or any liquid he managed to find in the closet ranging from white spirit to all-purpose cleaners.

We were trying to survive in this mayhem for a very long five years. And so did Mycobacterium tuberculosis in my wife's lungs[50]. The bug won and my wife went into hospital for an endless eleven months leaving me alone with a two-year-old son in conditions o f which Diogenes of Sinope would have been proud. I will continue looking at that particular problem through the prism most relevant to the topic of this story—getting a new flat. This approach generally helps to get you through things like that.

From several sources, I soon found out the key points I should use in my quest: (i) tuberculosis is generally considered a 'social' contagious disease and many famous Bolsheviks had it, such as Felix Dzerzhinsky[51] and Maxim Gorky[52] just to name a couple of THEM; (ii) in recognition of this problem, Lenin issued decrees which distinguished tuberculosis from other diseases, with patients receiving free hospital and sanatorium treatment and, most importantly in the context of this story, individual flats. We were also lucky in that my wife had an open form of tuberculosis, i.e. the one that could be transmitted to other people. The last point clinched the completely logical structure, and I began to make appointments to see two local authority representatives, let us call them X and Y, of the Soviet organs that dealt with the housing problem at the local and district level. They quite predictably spat and sneezed upon my face and wiped the floor with me, shouting that my family would rot in this filthy den forever and that we had no rights at all. Quod erat demonstrandum.

After this unavoidable purgatory, I methodically began to write letters – something at which that I turned out to be very good.

- *Letters? What letters?*
- *THE letters on behalf of my indignant neighbours!*

I was writing to all medical, sanitary, Soviet and communist party organs at the local, district, city and national levels on behalf of my neighbours who then kindly signed them (God, bless them!).

A typical letter of mine written on behalf of my neighbours would start with a proud citation or reminder that Lenin was fighting against the tsarist regime for the rights of ordinary people. Then it would draw the attention of the reader to the first decrees of the young Soviet Republic led by Lenin that guaranteed treatment and dwellings to isolate people with the most notorious social disease inherited from the rotten tsarist Empire, the disease that some of the most dedicated Russian revolutionaries died of (you know a couple of their names already) whilst defending all the proletariat in the world. This tragedy should not be repeated. However, my young family had an epicentre of this notorious disease that threatened the lives of three innocent babies (the two deranged bandits and one dark room philosopher mentioned above) from a proletarian family and WWII veterans who had fought for the communist party ideals to their last drop of blood. Therefore, we, the neighbours, could not understand the bizarre position of comrades X and Y who seemed not to appreciate the revolutionary achievements of the Soviet Union in combating the aftermath of the tsarist past thus undermining the generous domestic policy of the communist party of the Soviet Union.

My heart turned to stone; I decided to go to the end of this epistolary exercise, which, to my mind, would end with me writing to the next and last XXVII Communist party Congress, which was due to take place in March 1986. This was the end of the road, the only window for cases like ours to be noticed and processed. It was the bone that THEM would throw to us every five years, but this window of opportunity was not open for a long time, and I had to send my final letter by autumn…

My wife was diagnosed with tuberculosis in February 1985 and we got a new flat in May 1985. I was spared the pleasure of writing to their last party Congress after all. I was looking through this particular prism for so long and so intensely that I did manage to burn a hole not only through my heart, but also through the concrete wall leading all three of us into a new flat, just like Pinocchio[53] who managed to get into a magic world through a hole in a picture that he punctured with his nose. Our new flat was located in the western part of Moscow with all three windows facing the sunset, as if it was trying to tell us something. Maybe it was showing us a vector, a direction in which to move, crawl, diffuse, go, fly, bang our heads against, or just meticulously drill through, just to be able to go as far away as possible (I dreamed on New Zealand at that time).

Buying a reasonable one-bedroom flat in the periphery of Moscow, 2011 will cost you about two hundred thousand USD, i.e. fifty years' average salary of ten thousand roubles (~three hundred and fifty USD) per month. Renting one will lighten your wallet by thirty to forty thousand roubles (one thousand to one thousand two hundred USD) per month. If you are an immigrant from Tajikistan (I met one of them called Hassan in summer 2010), you would be lucky to clean streets for ten thousand roubles per month and live with your family in a ramshackle grubby basement decorated with communication cables, water pipes and cement floors. Your rent of five thousand roubles would be payable in an envelope directly to the Head of the local Housing Authority.

Municipal housing is currently available for Muscovites with an area quota below ten to fifteen m^2 per person depending on the particular district, with an average waiting time of about twenty years[54]. Obviously, the situation with municipal housing has not changed dramatically over the years.

However, not everything is so gloomy! If your income is five million roubles per year (about one hundred and seventy thousand USD) as in the recent criminal case of Mr. Bulanov[55], you will be able to accumulate sixty years' income (~one hundred million USD) and dramatically improve your living conditions. Mr. Bulanov showed great taste in his selection of the properties that he acquired all over world, including an elite cottage in the Moscow region, village Milukino; another mansion in village Shavoronki (~ ten million USD); a flat in the centre of Moscow (~ seven million USD); a garage cooperative; a flat in Paris, France (one and a half million euro) and in Nice, France (one and a half million euro); a private apartment block with fourteen luxury apartments (~ seventy-five million USD). In order to get to all these places, Mr. Bulanov's Yin and Yang[56] can drive simultaneously two luxury cars costing more than £100,000 each.

For some reason, Mr. Bulanov was sacked, his properties arrested and valuables confiscated. But why? Did not he share enough with those above him, or maybe he was too big for his boots and was up to an even larger acquisition?[57] Maybe one hundred million USD is an implicit top limit in their pecking order, and his second Jeep a last drop. Muscovites are confused as to what the problem was. Was Mr. Bulanov really so different from Mr Alpatov[58], who declared about 18 million roubles (0.6 million USD) as his annual income in 2009. Obviously, exclusively from this income he managed to buy six apartment blocks in Moscow with a combined area of 1,166,000 m^2, three elite flats of four hundred m^2, a cottage of 484 m^2, three luxury county houses, a church, topped off with a car, which you can only see at a car exhibition. Everyone is relieved to know that Mr. Alpatov is not corrupt. After all, there is wisdom in hard work and sharing the results of this work with the right people. It may also be of help to have relatives and/or protectors at a higher level of the pack.

Acquisition of islands by those seeking noble solitude for meditation, writing philosophical doctrines and studies of their souls became a new trend in the last few years. For example, an uninhabited island, Estonia seem to had attracted the philosophical attention and life savings of Mr. S. Matvienko (the son of St. Petersburg Mayor Mrs. V. Matvienko[59]), while Volgograd Mayor Mr. E. Ischenko seem to had always been drawn for entirely understandable and very human reasons to purchase an island in the Maldives, quite possibly for meditation purposes[60].

Did you hear in the last months or so about the interest of 'an undisclosed party' in acquiring the American continent? Someone must have a lot of meditating to do.

You Buy Vodka, But You Drink Vodochka!

Only vodka from Russia is genuine Russian vodka

-William Pokhlebkin

Vodka is a diminutive derived from the Russian word 'water' ('вода', 'voda') with an addition of the diminutive suffix '-k–'. Another diminutive from the same word 'Vodichka' still means 'water' (however, 'Vodochka' means 'vodka'). The quote refers to the unsubstantiated claims of Smirnoff and other American producers of a similar alcoholic drink that this term can be used by them and other "vodka" producers, such as those in Poland, Ukraine, Finland, Sweden etc. Characteristically, the above companies use boiled water, as well as different types of grain and distillation technologies, which result in a quite distinct chemical composition, look and taste of their alcoholic drink. Because of using fresh water, Russian vodka is crystal clear, or as we say, 'like a tear'. William Vasiljevich Pokhlebkin (1923-2000) is the author of 50 books including numerous culinary books and monographs, such as on the history of tea and vodka. 'A history of vodka' (late 1970s) is the most thorough monograph about this subject in the world that helped the Soviet Union to retain the monopoly on vodka production in the world at that time. Pokhlebkin is known also as an expert in the history of diplomacy and Russian international relations, a journalist and a geographer. His father was Russian revolutionary Vasili Mikhailov, who was known by his underground nickname of 'Pokhlebkin' (meaning 'stew'). William Pokhlebkin adopted his father's underground nickname as his penname. William Pokhlebkin was brutally killed in his apartment in Podolsk in March 2000, nothing was taken from the scene and the criminal case has never been solved.

By luck or by misfortune, by any means, we finally got a new flat in 1985, and I was preparing for the house-warming party. I decided to be generous and bought some vodka for the first time, as previously due to lack of money I had prepared home-made liquor from cherries and pure alcohol, which was of course illegal. I bought Moskovskaya Vodka because I knew that this brand was a gold standard, the best vodka in the world[61]. It was easy enough to calculate how many bottles I needed - one for every male guest. After I bought vodka it became vodochka (водочка) and should have been treated like a spoiled child with all due tenderness and care—one should check the lid for leakages, place it in the dark away from prying eyes, put it in the deep freezer one day before the event, plan the traditional hors d'oeuvres, snacks, salads and hot dishes that could be served optimally with vodochka. Russians treat vodochka almost like a child and even discuss everything about the vodochka ritual in the same language, as we might speak to a child. All words would be modified to acquire one of many Russian diminutive suffixes, as you might say to a child a doggie instead of a dog. Vodka acquires its typical diminutive suffix when it becomes yours and is readily available for the sacred ceremony of its consumption.

Over the years, I have heard a well-established stereotype in the West that Russian people drink a lot for the sake of drinking, that vodka is consumed by all people including women, children and so on. Nothing could be further from the truth, as for us this is a very complex and sophisticated ceremony, not unlike the Japanese tea ceremony. No one present would have the aim of getting drunk, quite the contrary; it is not about drinking at all! For us, it is being part of arguably the oldest tradition in the world[62], which still comforts our bodies and souls to this day. Drinking without being drunk – this would be the greatest possible achievement at the ceremonial table.

Let me give you a flavour of the rather intricate Russian drinking ceremony. First of all, not only 'vodka' would change its name as explained above, but also all items on the table, the dishes, cutlery, glasses, napkins, bread would only be addressed by your guests as if they had suddenly turned into children themselves. There would be no bread, but breaddie (хлебушек), no herring, but herringie (селедочка), no mere cucumbers, mushrooms or tomatoes – as if they had all shrunk for the children around the table to understand what you were referring to. The centre of the table universe is vodochka, or some people would still use the original pre-vodka words of the sixteenth and seventeenth centuries, such as wine (Вино), Brandakhlist (Брандахлыст) or white stuff (Беленькое).

Vodochka must be with a tear (со слезой) meaning with visible condensation of water running down from the ice-cold bottle. Ideally it should be accompanied with salted (not pickled) cucumbers (rather cucumberies, огурчики), salted herringies, mushroomies (грибочки) or frozen solid lard prepared with salt and garlic known as salo (сало) on slices of rye breadie.

People would never rush, because rushing would be considered very bad style and a sign of disrespect. Everything would proceed in a strict order, drinking would be frequently accompanied by light background music such as guitar, vivid conversation with a lot of jokes, humour and funny stories. To keep the ball rolling would be one of the important tasks of the host, and he or the other guests would gently interrupt the general conversation with highly eloquent toasts and addresses. The toasts and their sequence would differ according to the particular occasion, such as a birthday or house warming. At the end of the toast, glasses would clink at all occasions except for remembering the dead. The role of the host and the host would also be to make everyone feel at home, and I have witnessed precedents when on expressing their delight about a particular object in the house, this object was immediately given to the admirer as a gift. I will stop here without going into too much further detail of the ceremony, including a 'penalty glass of vodochka for the last to arrive and the last glass of vodochka before departure called na pososhok (на посошок, on the walking stick.)

Our guests were beginning to arrive fashionably late, which the unwritten politeness codex says is thirty minutes after the agreed time, neither too early nor too late. Bringing flowers for the host and a bottle of wine for the host was obligatory. It was considered bad tone for the host to open the bottles you just got from a guest, as if you did not care to prepare everything beforehand. Since this was a house-warming party, we were getting all sorts of small things for the kitchen, pots of flowers, plates for traditional Russian pelmeni[63] and so on.

The table was laid with one notable exception—vodochka was still in its comfortable freezer cradle. The Sleeping Beauty was getting thicker and thicker every moment, ripening in this frost like an olive under the generous Mediterranean sun to produce a drink of life.[64] It would be there until the very last minute, until the host was kind enough to present the baby to the public. If you happened to be the guest, you could not possibly ask about the You-Know-What, that would be rude – as you had not come here to drink. You could only sit and wait for the sun (rather sunnie) to appear from behind the clouds.

I quickly fetched the Liquid Centre of the Universe. This was the key moment, a moment of truth – would it be accepted? Could you clearly see the precious tear running from the white bottle, from the glass (rather glassie, рюмочка, ideally about 50 ml in volume) and from the eyes of at least some of the guests? We called those tears a miserly masculine tear' ('скупая мужская слеза').

I never drank the first 'glassie', I just had some water to see how people reacted to the toast 'To our meeting' (За встречу), how the metal would melt in their eyes, their tongues lose their stiffness. In any case, the time between the first and the second toast was usually very short[65]...

- *Could you actually drink at your own pace not adhering to any toasts?*
- *No, you could not. You could propose a toast, and then everyone was supposed to drink. If you felt you wanted to have a break after a while, it was okay to stop drinking early.*

Dancing, going for a walk, singing and/or listening to someone playing the guitar also belonged to the ceremonial steps accommodated naturally in between the cold and hot dishes, before dessert or after tea. The whole thing would usually take the entire day with the guests leaving to catch the last metro around midnight, with some tough soldiers remaining on the battlefield fighting until the last bullet and the last drop of blood.

Russians are very tough people with very vulnerable souls. Everyone knows that alcohol is used widely to clean fine optics. In Russia, it is used to clean the optics of our souls from many, too many tough people without any soul at all. THEM drink to get drunk, to drown their conscience in vodka and then to do whatever they want with us and Russia – revolutions, their communist nonsense, but in essence quite materialistically to pump our resources into their bottomless pockets or even to destroy us altogether just like they had previously destroyed the Byzantine Empire[66]...

I even suspect that THEM would go as far as to dare refer to our 'vodochka' by the vulgar word 'vodka' – something that any normal Russian would never do.

How is our vodochka doing in Moscow, 2011? Let us start with some statistics. According to World Health Organisation (WHO) data, alcohol consumption in Russia is more than double (18 litres) the critical level set by WHO at eight litres of spirit per year per person including babies[67]. Official data suggest that 2.3 million people in Russia are alcoholics, while unofficially this number is thought to be about five million, i.e. one in twenty-nine people[68].

Reflecting on the current situation in Moscow, I noticed that people do not tend to invite friends to their homes anymore and prefer to go out for a quick or not-so-quick drink to a bar or restaurant. The vodochka tradition is dying out, and I am starting to observe people referring to this drink as plain vodka. Vodka remains very cheap, and one can buy a half litre bottle for nineteen roubles[69] (~0.6 US dollars). Hence, an average monthly salary of ten thousand roubles (~three hundred and thirty US dollars) would buy you about two hundred and sixty-three litres of cheap vodka in Moscow of today, whereas twenty-five years ago it would have been only 15 litres (the average salary was one hundred and twenty roubles per month, and the cheapest vodka was ~four roubles per 0.5 l)!

Whatever THEM are trying to achieve by encouraging people to drink themselves under the table, this pro-alcoholic state policy is very effective at targeting the Russian population from an epidemiological point of view. Indeed, according to Russian epidemiologists, alcohol is responsible for more than 50% deaths in Russia[70]. The drastic changes in socio-economic factors after 1991 resulted in a surge of alcoholism, an abrupt reduction in the quality of life and a long-lasting population decline in Russia (the population of Russia fell by 6 million people between 1995-2010[71]). To compensate for the loss of the Russian population of nearly 1 million per year, about 1.3million immigrants of non-Russian origin from the southern former Soviet states immigrate to Russia every year[72]. In contrast, only 900 ethnic Russian immigrants were registered in 2008[73].

This targeted state policy changes the demographic composition of Russia, the quality of spoken Russian language and the distribution of various religious confessions in Russian society. A prognosis carried out by the UN predicts that by 2050 the population of Russia will be 98 million (down from the current 142 million[74]), within which ethnic Russians will become a minority by the mid 21 century[75], akin to the not-dissimilar predictions of Dr. Zbigniew Brzezinski on Russia becoming empty one day.[76]

Speaking to the British elite on November 17 2008,[77] Dr. Brzezinski said, "It is easier to kill a million people than it is to control them". THEM made this discovery much earlier and successfully applied it throughout Soviet and modern Russian history. The dwindling of the Russian population at a rate of about 1 million per year proves that you do not need gulags to achieve this goal. What you need to do instead is to the kill faith, pride, hope and trust of the people... and instil unadulterated alcoholism on a population-wide scale.

No Tea – No Communism!

If you don't drink tea, where do you get your strength from?

- Popular Russian saying

"Where there's tea, there's hope"

- a slogan from a poster by Whittard of Chelsea

I have always been a serious tea drinker, and it was a bit of a challenge to sustain this simple habit in Moscow, 1985. It may or may not be one of the reasons why we eventually emigrated along the more traditional and stable tea route to England. On my first visit to the dentist, my tea-drinking habit was immediately spotted on taking just a quick look at my teeth.

- *Oh, you are a heavy tea drinker, Sir...Believe me, I have seen plaque before, but for the first time they are of the colour of tea!*

As you can imagine, this innocent habit of ours has flourished in Albion, the country widely associated with tea, and guests coming to our house are always surprised by the variety of different loose leaf teas on offer. My wife and I have become tea gourmets; we are always bringing new sorts of tea back from our various travels, receiving gifts of tea from friends and friends of friends, always looking for better tea pots, better tea cups, better tea caddies. We leave tap water to settle for at least a day before using it for brewing tea, never allow the kettle to over-boil, cover the teapot with a linen towel during the brewing process – all in anticipation of the magic of good tea!

In Moscow, 1985, you could not buy teabags, and I was introduced to my first teabag in my thirties in Germany. Tea has always been a bit of a cult in Russia, with many Russian painters, such as Vasily Perov[78], Ivan Kulikov[79] and Boris Kustodiev[80] picturing tea drinking parties and ceremonies in the Russian Empire amongst various social classes.

Tea arrived to Russia in the 16th century when Siberian Cossacks brought this exotic drink to the Russian tsar and court directly from China. By the beginning of the twentieth century, the Russian Empire was <u>the</u> most tea-drinking nation[81], consuming more tea than any other country in the world. Most tea came from China including some very expensive and unique yellow tea varieties, the export of which was normally regarded as a criminal offence in China. Those teas were unavailable in other countries and were exported exclusively to Russia for the Emperor's family and the Court via a barter exchange system for the most rare and expensive Siberian furs, such as stoat and sable. In fact, nearly two thirds of the entire Russian fur production was at one point being exchanged for Chinese tea. Merchants trading tea belonged to the richest and most influential of the Russian business elite, and trading the first packet of tea served as an official start of the most important annual market in Nizhny Novgorod[82].

Drinking tea, and primarily black tea, was an expensive and prestigious pastime in Russia[83] before the Revolution. It is not clear why, but this habit was quickly adopted by many Russian people by the end of the 19th century and was placed right in the centre of our culture, tradition, language and even the military ration from 1886. It is still the case that if you give a tip, say, to a taxi driver or in a restaurant, you would call it tea-money (чаевые) or literally for tea (на чай). Right from the start, the attitude of Russians to tea has always been as affectionate and tender as to vodka, or rather vodochka, such that similar diminutive suffixes were used to describe desserts that go well with tea, such as jammie (вареньице) instead of jam (варенье), or cakie (тортик) rather than cake (торт) and so on. The tea (чай) itself would transform into tea-ie (чаёк) – all to make you feel relaxed and content. The tea tradition in Russia has developed independently of the European style, such that it dictates that desserts should be served together with tea and not before, as in most Western countries. Therefore, if you wanted to ask what was for dessert or pudding, you would ask what was available with tea' (к чаю).

By the mid-1980s, the richness of the tea culture in Moscow was gone and the best black tea we could dream of was a generic Indian tea with three elephants on the packet, which is why we called it 'Three elephants'. Incidentally, the label and unofficial name of this tea were quite right, as indeed it was similar in its aroma to three elephants. Many people including myself sought other options, and quite unexpectedly, we found that at that time the Soviet Union was still producing some reasonable sorts of black tea and the quality of their blends was close to Chinese tea! Therefore, these so-called Russian teas were progressively gaining in popularity in the country and abroad, not for long though[84]. I actually quite liked some of the Georgian teas, such as Extra with a characteristic strong and pleasant tea flavour, colour and texture. It was a wonderful tea, indeed. As far as I am concerned, they should have kept the tea plantations in Georgia over the vineyards...

One of the most interesting questions about tea is why it always played such a pivotal role in the economic and political processes in tea-drinking countries, such as Russia and the USA. THEM know the answer, as they seem to have been painfully aware of this importance of tea in Russian culture and everyday life. Straight after the October Revolution in the middle of the civil war, one of Lenin's first decrees was to establish a separate Tea Ministry called Centrochai (Центрочай, Centre of Tea), which was to deal with all aspects of the tea business, including its purchase, distribution and consumption all over Russia. Even in the most dangerous and difficult times, tea supply was maintained at constant levels, being as important as ammunition, bread, salt, tobacco and vodka.

- *Why is it that tea was apparently so important? I am sure Lenin had more important things on his mind during that time...*

- *I do not know for sure, but Lenin would have been aware of the Boston Tea Party of 1773. That revolt started initially against the tea monopoly of the British East-India Company and resulted not only in the unfortunate destruction of that particular tea cargo, but also initiated the American Revolution and separation of the USA from Britain. Understandably, they did not want to repeat this mistake in Russia...*

The American and Russian examples show clearly that tea-drinking people would go as far as revolutions, wars, riots just to secure a nice cup of tea. It is impossible to explain to someone who does not drink it... How should I say? Drinking tea makes you happy, strong, healthy, it boosts your self-esteem, it warms you up in freezing winters and cools you down in scorching summers, it reduces your appetite and makes you slimmer, it opens your heart (and coronary vessels) to understanding the essence and philosophy of life, it stops time and closes the space around that magic brown brew.

THEM did not want to make us happy and they got rid of tea by the end of 1980s altogether! What THEM did not expect though was that it would lead to obvious repercussions comparable to the Boston Tea party and culminate in the breakdown of the Soviet Union. Russian people just reckoned that there was no point in tolerating the regime without tea!

What a feast! What a variety of tastes, colours and qualities of teas sold in plastic or cartons, cans, vacuum packs, or by weight in Moscow, 2011! Particularly abundant are green teas – our favourites. If I said above that 50% of the space in small supermarkets was occupied by vodkas, probably at least twenty to twenty-five percent is devoted to teas. Exotic names, such as Milk Ulun, Dragon's Whiskers or Green Snail immerse you in a pure nirvana of anticipation and joy. Prices are surprisingly quite affordable, particularly in the markets. Black teas are a bit of a problem being more expensive and unpredictable in quality and taste. It could be to do with deterioration of the water quality in Moscow, 2011, which was much better twenty-five years ago, such that most people now use filtered water for making tea. We have remained a non tea bag family, so tea bags are beyond the scope of this story.

If you go out in Moscow, 2011, you will be most certainly served a teapot of brewed leaf tea; prices are at least double which you might expect. However, if you want you can reproduce any of the tea drinking compositions from the paintings mentioned above. Just a few words of warning – you will not find a reasonable espresso in the usual tourist haunts... I must acknowledge that THEM have finally drawn the lessons from the Boston Tea party! At least from the tea perspective THEM are safe!

To a Light Steam!

"In the banya and in a queue all people are equal"

-a popular saying in mid 1980s

"To a light steam" is a common Russian saying to someone going to the banya. By saying that, we express a highly polite hope that on this particular occasion the steam was not too heavy and did not cause nausea or headache, but that on the contrary it was healthy, light and pleasant leaving the person happy and enlightened after the banya experience. There are numerous jokes, aphorisms and sayings about the Russian sauna or banya. Many people in Russia treat the banya tenderly from the same perspective as drinking vodochka or tea. This is not surprising because the Russian word banya is related to the Latin balneum (bathing house). Senators in ancient Rome used to lie in the balneum and discuss important issues, drink wine and enjoy themselves in various other ways. This is the easiest, most obvious and popular interpretation of what the banya is about. In essence, this point of view maintains that in the banya people wash away the physical dirt and enjoy themselves. This is, of course, true!

However, it is not the whole story, and I daresay that the banya was also designed to teach us wash away our metaphysical dirt, so-to-speak. In this respect, I like to believe that the banya concept was developed by the Apostle St. Andrew who preached in ancient Russia as far north as the Volga river and the city of Kiev (now part of the Ukraine), and became a patron saint of Russia and, interestingly, Scotland[85]. Could that explain why Russian and Scottish people get along so well? In any case, when St. Andrew visited Novgorod he was bewildered by the observation that Russians were *lashing themselves so violently that they barely got out alive* and it was probably he who filled this seemingly senseless entertainment with deep religious content.

- *Is all this just theory, or did you used to go to banya yourself on a regular basis?*

- *Yes, I used to go to the most famous banya in Moscow called Sanduni !*

My friend Oleg and I used to go to the banya together, and we met some amazing people there. They were banya professionals, so they did not talk much, but they were good at making sure the steam was light! I suspect they used to spent all day doing that, and it was completely and purely on a voluntary basis. They took care of the heart of the banya – the steam-room: they cleaned and ventilated it, they would bring some special oils and instruments for this, they controlled the occupancy of the steam-room. Those professionals would show how to use the bunch of dry birch twigs (venik) – something that St. Andrew took to be a senseless torturing instrument in Novgorod so many years ago. Their power over the steam-room was absolute. For a good reason they could expel you, but they could also endow you with a banya knighthood (valid for one visit only) and give you the right to pour some of the complex fragrant mixture onto the hot stones. Seeing the respect in their eyes was as precious as the Crown jewels.

- *Please tell us a bit about this seemingly complicated banya ritual.*

- *Anyone who practises martial arts would tell you that, for example, karate is "a way of cognition of life". So is banya. I had probably achieved no more than a yellow belt in the art of banya, so I cannot tell you much. Technically, I would make three to four short steam-room visits interspaced with progressively longer periods of time. There was almost no time gap between the first and second visit, then a few minutes lying in ice-cold water between two and three, then a relatively long break between three and four with a single gulp of water, and then I would allow myself a last short breath of light steam. Time spent in the steam-room was particularly precious. The task was to get your cold and dirty guts to become as warm and clean as soon as possible, hopefully within the first two visits. Lashing with the "venik" did help remove the internal filth and cold, but this instrument needed to be used very wisely, like a painter's brush.*

Working with the venik was very complicated. First, it needed to be revived from its dry sleep by being soaked in boiling water during the first steam-room visit. Then it needed to compare the lightness of the steam with the roughness of your skin during the second visit to figure out the best way to help you. This step was obviously shorter if you happened to use it for the second and last time, because your venik would remember the previous experience. Upon escaping from the steam-room, each time the venik should be caressed back into the boiling water waiting for the pinnacle of its livelihood – the third main visit to the steam-room, when you are lashed to what feels like death, which is necessary to transfer the energy of the sun accumulated in its tender revitalised leaves into your body.

I clearly remember the end of my short banya spell in the cold winter of 1985. On that particular occasion, the steam decided to be particularly light on me. I was on top form, my highly elaborate sequence of actions in and out of the steam-room was impeccable, and I was even allowed to sprinkle a bit of eucalyptus water onto white-hot stones. As a result, I was flying as light and airy as a feather on the way back to the Metro station still called Revolution Square. I literally could not feel my legs, or the rest of my body. My disembodied mind, thoughts and soul were united in clean happiness, I felt no distress, and I was hovering above Moscow in a state of ethereal nirvana…

However, if you happened to live in Moscow then, even on the highest peak of your religious, metaphysical or creative revelation, in the crescendo of your eureka moment, during the most profound spell of pure joy and happiness - one could not forget about the militia men that usually liked to patrol around every Metro station. We all knew that for some reason THEM profoundly hated seeing any happy glowing faces, which probably made THEM suspicious of state treason or some kind of plot against THEM. Therefore, I needed to reluctantly come back to Earth and do something to persuade THEM that I was as unhappy as everyone else, that I was clean from conspiracy against the state.

Just before entering the Metro station, I grabbed a handful of dirty snow and stuffed it underneath my collar to make sure my facial expression adjusted to their own and more in line with their expectations.

Banyas have become private, the steam-rooms are usually mediocre, the professionals are gone and replaced with all sorts of Thai massages, *have a nice traditional Russian banya with taste* or more direct offers in Moscow, 2011. Militia men (if your skin colour is white and if you do not look directly into their eyes) reluctantly tolerate the happy expressions of people after banyas. In all other cases, make sure you have your passport ready for inspection.

Generally speaking, people in Moscow of today do not seem to be getting joy from traditional and simple pastimes, be it tea drinking, going to banya, going for a walk, meeting a friend, enjoying the sunset, inviting guests round, playing with a child, drinking our vodochka properly or just singing in the evenings, which to my great surprise people still do in Venice, Italy, for example. Does this mean that the mere interest in life is decreasing and people are trying to compensate it with money and other material commodities? Was it really so necessary *to destroy everything to the ground, and then build a new, a better world*[86]...?

This seems to be the right time to ask THEM – what now, what kind of a better world are you going to create, when and for whom?

Flowers in the Swamp

"The family is the essential cell of society"

-a popular Soviet slogan

There were many swamps around Moscow, 1985, which is very convenient from a number of different points of view. Firstly, swamps protected Moscow from invasions, as they had done during the Napoleonic Wars and later during World Wars I and II. Secondly, EVERYTHING dissolves and burns in the peaty swamps, from bodies to memories. I can assure you that this property of the swamps was used extremely effectively. Finally, peat can be used for fertilising soil and therefore there is an ocean of beautiful flowers in swamps around Moscow. You will not find better flowers anywhere else in the world. Why so?

For one reason or another, my great-aunt was not allowed to live in Moscow. THEM could have just killed her, for example, because of her baroness title, or because she had graduated from the Smolny Institute of Noble Maidens, St. Petersburg[87]. Well, I am saying that just in case THEM needed a reason to kill people, which they do not. Instead, after her graduation they generously selected a swampy village for her dwelling for the rest of her life. What was the deal between her and THEM? She never actually told anyone about her ordeal. I do not remember much from my childhood, but I do remember her visiting us once in Moscow. Perhaps it was some important family occasion. I do not think that she just wanted to have lovely afternoon tea with the family because she was so scared that she rushed back as soon as she could. After this afternoon tea, she started to limp on her left leg and needed a walking stick. This was the only occasion that I remember her going further than the bus stop in this swampy village. I think she must have chosen this life in exchange for THEM not touching the rest of us. It worked, THEM did not touch us, THEM just tried to kill our family's memory and pride in the swamp.

In the early 1980s when I was in my early twenties, I liked to cross-country ski with my dad to this swampy village and then have some boiled potatoes, bread, salted cabbage and pickled cucumbers for lunch. I could not usually think clearly after a few hours of skiing at minus 20-30 ° C, so it was a bit of a boring murmur about our relatives who immigrated to France after the Revolution, about the genealogy of our family, which I was supposed to learn, and which I was not supposed to make any written notes of. I have always disappointed her, which I regret very much. It was a poor excuse that at that time all the distinguished members of the family who served Russian tsars before the Revolution, sounded like swamp delirium. Due to a lack of diligence, I would usually get a hit on the forehead with a wooden spoon and then drift off to a deep sleep.

Our family does not have any written documents, photographs, or in fact anything tangible, left in the family on many, many, many family members and distinguished Russian citizens, who had built railways, supplied water to Moscow, fought in many wars, written poetry... all unfortunately at the wrong time – i.e. BEFORE the Revolution! All archives had been burned or maybe were just destroyed by the all-forgiving swamps around Moscow by the last baroness? No one has any memoirs or notes left of any kind more substantial than an ice-cream recipe, because the patriarchs wanted to save their children. We suddenly became a Russian family, not a German family, as it was considered before the Revolution, because we all wanted to save our children and did everything to achieve this.

My great-aunt died in 1985 in the swamp village squalid hospital, which was just a simple house filled with desperate old people. When we visited her for the last time, she was smiling at me and my three-year old son – her mission was over. We were not allowed to give her a decent burial, and she was buried in an unmarked collective grave in the swamp. After her death I am keeping her legacy – a samovar, a retirement present of the swamp Peat Factory collective, and a collection of unsigned blank postcards from many European countries dated from 1917-1920. The first thing I did was to methodically destroy the letters from our French relatives, all photographs and other documents I could find - we all need to keep our children safe after all...

The swamps change with the season. If you ski over their icy surfaces in winter, you do not feel the deadly power below. In spring, however, swamps will produce the best flowers in the world – these are all individual human memories, photographs of your baby, smiles, broken hearts and legs and other treasures hidden away there, but not destroyed. Therefore, the swamps around Moscow are covered with tapestries of billions and billions of beautiful flowers. I must give THEM that - they tried their very best to create this phenomenon.

The flowers around Moscow, 2011, are still there, all right! They will always surround Moscow until our universe implodes back into a minute super dense mass of primordial material or these flowers will intertwine themselves into a funeral wreath on the grave of THEM.

There was a big fire in the swamps around Moscow were burning in summer 2010, pointing in the direction of nature and/or God being against THEM. Whatever is hidden there reached a critical mass, and the deepest and strongest forces in the universe started their fight against THEM. The Russian writer D. S. Merezhkovsky[88] was considering this struggle to be between Christ and Anti-Christ, and the outcome is not clear yet.

A Minute of Silence

"Brezhnev addressed the Politburo: - Comrades! We have a situation where many members of the Politburo have slipped into senility; they play games, ride wooden horses... But Kosygin went too far, he took away my tin solders and refuses to give THEM back (sobs)... "

-a popular joke in the 1980s

In the joke above Alexey Nikolaevich Kosygin (1904-1980), member of the Politburo of the Central Committee of the communist party of the Soviet Union (1948-1980), President of the Council of Ministers of the Soviet Union (1964-1980). Kosygin tried to introduce economic reforms, which were not supported at his time and laid the foundations for the Perestroika reforms of M. S. Gorbachev.

The Secretary-General of the communist party of the Soviet Union Leonid Ilyich Brezhnev died on 10 November 1982 having been in power for 18 years. He took over the reign from Nikita Khrushchev on 14 October 1964 and surrendered it to the KGB head Yuri Andropov. One can easily argue that this is still the case today. As we used to joke at the dawn of the KGB reign,

"the sexual revolution had happened in Russia at last because the organs took power".

I remember Brezhnev's demise, the following four days of nationwide mourning and his funeral on 15 November 1982 when all roads in Moscow were closed. It was time of total and utter silence and blackout. THEM managed to stop time for those endless five days without any work, news, television and radio. All TV channels were showing either movies about the October Revolution, Lenin and other great Bolsheviks or the classic ballet by P.I. Tchaikovsky, Swan Lake. There was not so much traffic in the streets, and all people outside seemed scared and perplexed. It was understandable, as Brezhnev was in power longer than anyone else before him, except for Joseph Stalin, and our generation knew only him, got used to him and his rules of the game. All my years at school, university and the first years at work were decorated with his omnipresent portraits, his passionate collection of all possible State rewards and Orders[89], and expensive cars (a humble collection of about 50 exemplars), his personality cult and his writing career[90]. After being choked by the obligatory discussions of his books in the collective meetings, we used to joke that

> "In the event of Brezhnev's death, bury him deep in Virgin land, cover him with Small land (soil), but spare us his 'Renaissance!'

Even if you made a public speech after defending your thesis, you were supposed to say something to the effect of:

> -   *Please allow me now to express gratitude to my scientific supervisor, to my colleagues, to the Scientific Committee, the Director, and in particular my thanks go to the Communist Party of the Soviet Union and personally to its greatest son – the Secretary-General Comrade Leonid Ilyich Brezhnev!*

All of us lived through those endless five days in a cloud of uncertainty and fear, we did not know what to expect or what would happen to us in the future. There was a complete information blockade, a paralysis of the entire country; it was like not knowing what was going on with your loved one who happened to be in the A&E ward. It did not matter how long you stared at Brezhnev's portrait looking at you from everywhere, you could not get any clue as to who was going to be next in line for nor what his course was likely to be. The situation reminded us of when THEM bravely abandoned Moscow in October 1941 as the German armies were looking at the Kremlin through their field binoculars[91].

It was much easier to get a grip after the demise of Andropov[92] and then Chernenko[93] who succeeded Brezhnev to stay in power for the next three years. You could imagine that there were many jokes about the rapid theatrical appearances of the party leaders on the political stage such as:

death row or

no-one wanted to die (the title of a well-known Russian movie).

However, this came much later. In those five days, we did not anticipate that Andropov's broom would remove twenty percent of the Secretaries of the Provincial Committee (in essence, the governors) for corruption and even look attentively at Brezhnev's clan. Nor did we know about the last desperate campaign for work discipline awaiting us in just a few days' time, when KGB officers started patrolling the streets of Moscow and checking if people had legitimate reasons not to be at work, which looked like the return of Stalin's rule to us. We had not yet witnessed genial plans of the communist party Secretary-General Mr. Chernenko to make the rivers in Siberia run in the opposite direction obviously in a vain hope that it would make things better. The saddest thing is that I am not joking about any of those plans; they did exist and were put into action!

At the end of the four-day nationwide mourning, I remember looking out of the window during Brezhnev's funeral and for a few minutes seeing no cars or people on the street whatsoever. I seriously thought it must be the end of the world, and in a way it was, the end of the communist sand castle. Brezhnev was right about not doing anything drastic to the castle because as soon as it was touched, it would collapse.

Then there was a minute of silence followed by long sirens in commemoration of his death, and everything was over. I know now that stones thrown by Brezhnev's fans during those commemoration sirens had broken many train windows, I know that his coffin was dropped into the grave as if to speed up the procedure, I know that everything tangible that Brezhnev had - cars, properties, cottages - was confiscated and/or given to other great Bolsheviks. It seems even THEM cannot take all this with THEM to the grave?

Honestly, even now I do not like the ballet 'Swan Lake' because it reminds me of Brezhnev's death, but worse the agony, uncertainty and information vacuum imposed on us in November 1982. As it turned out, all police, militia, KGB, army and Special Forces were working round the clock on high alert at the time. What were they afraid of? That we would go out into the streets to demand Brezhnev's body to be put in a mausoleum? Or maybe quite rightly they were afraid of the innocent souls of all Russian people butchered during his reign who could potentially scream inappropriately during that solemn minute of silence, like in the famous novel and movie 'The Silence of the Lambs'?

Great men are considered great because they did a lot for their country. What is it that drives THEM to serve themselves? One can spend one hundred million dollars being at the Prefect of the Moscow region level[94], but cannot possibly spend three billion US dollars at the Moscow Mayor level[95], and who knows how much at the very top.

Alexander the Great established the largest empire in ancient history, and his ego, charisma and military talent were beyond comparison. His greatness has engraved itself in Greek and non-Greek mythology as a classical hero in the form of Achilles. In addition to his legendary military victories in the conquered regions, his greatness brought about the appearance of a new Hellenistic culture which affected Byzantine culture up to the 15th century. I am sure that when he died there was a different siren and eternal minute of silence commemorating his achievements up to the present day.

At the end of the day, what will THEM leave behind with the exception of swamps and long sirens?

Fear

Gorbachev ended the Cold War, destroyed the Iron Curtain, withdrew troops from Afghanistan, freed us from fear.!

- Article 'There will be no comeback of the authoritarian rule', newspaper 'Novije Izvestija', 02.03.06

Mikhail Sergeyevich Gorbachev (DOB, 2 March 1932), the Secretary-General of the communist party of the Soviet Union (11.03.1985-23.08.1991), the first Russian President (15.03.1990-25.12.1991), Nobel Prize winner for Peace (1990) who initiated the 'Perestroika' – the series of profound reforms of the political, economical and ideological system in the Soviet Union. His activity was interrupted by Boris Yeltsin who dissolved the Soviet Union in order to gain power in the Russian Federation. Gorbachev has nearly disappeared from the political scene now, such that even his 75th birthday was not publicly celebrated.

Not so long ago, my wife and I were looking through our family photographs and noticed the appearance of fear in the eyes of our son from a certain age. According to these photographs, the expression of fear was not present in his eyes until about the age of five or six years, when children usually acquire intellectual abilities.

- *This is, of course, very interesting and sad. Why would children in Moscow, 1985 become chronically scared from such an early age?*
- *According to child psychologists, fear can destroy or damage intellectual abilities in some children. This fact seems to be a good explanation of why THEM felt they had to start turning people into zombies from kindergarten age. Apparently, they have little demand for intellectual people.*
- *So how did they actually do it?*

- *I never dared to ask my son. My own kindergarten memories are quite unpleasant in this regard, and I simply cannot write about it.*

The result was that Russian people constantly had a pronounced, deep and conspicuous expression of fear in their eyes until about the mid-1990s, which would make us stand out in the crowd everywhere. Thanks to Gorbachev, this expression of fear wore off over time and it is much less obvious now in the new millennium. This feeling of being vulnerable and unprotected resided in our subconscious, and therefore was invisible to us, but for an outside observer we looked like trapped animals.

- *If you cannot tell us much about your childhood memories, could you at least describe for us what exactly you were afraid of as a grown-up?*
- *The answer to that question can be found throughout this book...*

For example, when I was reading The Gulag Archipelago by A. Solzhenitsyn, I felt as if someone was always watching me and that I was in serious danger, which in any case was an objective fact... At work, I was totally dependent on my immediate manager and the Director who could do with me whatever they pleased. Similar power was bestowed on any militia officer on the street, who could detain and beat people half dead for no reason at all...

Unfortunately, I am not exaggerating. I looked a bit Jewish, and anti-Semitism was, alas, a key feature of the Soviet regime... I had descended from an old non-proletarian family, which was never an advantage in the USSR... I was unusual in the way I perceived and thought about things around me, and quite dangerously for me, other people could read that from my face... I asked all sorts of unnecessary questions... Knowing my weak points, I did not feel confident that my face would always show what was expected to be seen. In Britain, even if you spoke in a posh aristocratic accent and then just one sound slipped out pronounced the way you used to, it would be noticed and appropriate conclusions about your origins would be drawn. It was in a way similar in the USSR – you were always on thin ice!

So obviously, we feared THEM, but we also feared our peers, as anyone could be an official or unofficial informant working for the KGB. Not everyone was a hidden dissident, like me, and there had been quite a few real believers who were also extremely dangerous. Leon Trotsky apparently had quite similar observations, which he published in *The Revolution betrayed. What is the Soviet Union and where is it going?* (1936), and he knew the subject all too well. As Trotsky had put it,

> Taught by bitter experience, the natural scientists, mathematicians, philologists, military theoreticians, would fear the "red professor", usually an ignorant careerist, who would threateningly pick on them with some quotation dragged from Lenin or Stalin. To defend one's own thought in such circumstances, or one's scientific dignity, means in all probability to bring down repressions upon one's head.

The problem of fear was not exclusively ours, and it had other vectors as well. Sometimes you would be able to detect fear in the eyes of the bureaucrats, too. This applied to situations when the Soviet political elite found themselves in unknown territory and did not know what exactly was expected of THEM. I clearly remember one American unemployed person – a Joe Mauri who, as a bizarre propaganda tool, was taken for a free tour through Russia in 1985 in exchange for his suspiciously well-articulated criticism of the West and favourable appraisal of life in the USSR. Each of Joe's step was fully documented, and thus we saw how Joe visited a huge metallurgical plant in Siberia. The almighty director, who clearly belonged to the highest stratum of the Soviet Nomenklatura[96], obviously was not briefed on how he should behave, not given any concrete directive on what to say or do, and so he had this all too familiar look of fear in his eyes. It looked as though he also might have had his own reasons to feel fear after all. It looked like an astonishing discovery to me, which I could not explain to myself at the time.

The solution to this apparent contradiction between THEM being in absolute control and still feeling the same or even stronger fear came to me again from reading Trotsky. Apparently, the

Soviet regime was based upon fear, and THEM had their own reasons to be afraid, too. Some of those reasons were quite obvious, such as falling out of favour or out of political context, which would effectively terminate their individual existence. In addition, according to Trotsky, the Soviet Nomenklatura were also afraid of *us* and of *our* intellectual criticism because this would threaten their own wellbeing – i.e. something that THEM came to power for in the first place!

Let me demonstrate this thought using a prehistoric metaphor of a hunting tribe with the happy fearless hunters coming back to the home cave with a slain mammoth. Everyone would get their fair share of the mammoth steak, which gave everyone an equal opportunity in their struggle for survival. Then at some point in human history, THEM evolved. For whatever reason, THEM did not hunt, THEM did not produce anything, THEM did not look after the fire or bring up children, THEM just consumed mammoth steaks. However, in order to be able to consume even more, THEM did produce one thing - the communist doctrine. Then THEM went to the trouble of organising a revolution and killing not only all the hunters, but also those who asked unnecessary questions. After a while, no one was left to ask any questions anymore, and THEM could consume as much as they liked, but they were still constantly terrified that someone might still be hiding behind the woodwork of their rotten structure... The more afraid they were, the crueler they became. As Stalin put it,

Strike your own people – it will make others fear!

Another aspect of the Soviet regime of fear was, of course, the fear of the Soviet Union by the West. This fear is still somewhat alive due to the often-unpredictable behaviour of Russian politicians and the lack of their international accountability. This is understandable – THEM are busy building a new Moscow, 2011 with a new rhetoric and new rituals, and the new cement laid on the old foundations has not dried yet.

Fear of Russia should not be associated with the country or its people, but with THEM. Russia was always there to protect the West from their growing appetites, and it will be always there for you... well, as long as a single mammoth hunter is still alive. The Russian people have nothing to do with THEM, we are simply hunters bringing home mammoths to be fairly shared by all.

Russian President Mr. Medvedev is currently lobbying for visa-free travel in Europe for Russians at the highest political international levels. In this respect, it is also useful to know that 70% Russians (i.e. 99.3 of the 141.8 million living in Russia[97]) are keen to leave the country, and they would do so if it was possible[98]. Mr. Medvedev's proposition implies that THEM do not need Russian people anymore, but this is only half of the story. The second half is that we never know what is going to be inside this Trojan horse.

Our fears were well defined twenty-five years ago, but the situation has since changed, so did THEM their tactics and our associated fears. If they expand in any direction, then there is a good reason behind that. Expansion northbound means exploring almost endless reserves of gas and oil, southbound – more new gas and oil pipelines, nuclear power stations, weapons and wars to be able to control territories of interest; westbound – more pipelines, drugs, smuggling children and prostitutes, criminal gangs, radioactive poisons, arms including biological weapons and, of course, buying, buying and buying more and more islands, real estate, political parties, football clubs, politicians, etc.

The bad news is that the Russian people can no longer protect the West from THEM metastasising in the westbound direction.

Cold

"Previously a Chukchi had two feelings: a sense of hunger and cold; now a Chukchi has a whole three feelings: a sense of hunger, cold and profound gratitude to the Soviet regime"

-a humorous answer of a Chukchi to the question: "What did the Soviet regime give to the Chukchi?"

Chukchi people (Чукчи) are ingenious people living in the coldest areas of Russia: the Chukchi Peninsula, the shores of the Arctic Ocean and Bering See. For one reason or another, Chukchi were the innocent targets of a series of popular jokes in the 1980s, similar to the kind of reciprocal jokes that exist between English and Irish or Scottish people

During winter, I was always cold. My head was fine because I had a rabbit fur hat, but my feet and hands were particularly suffering. I am not saying that the rest of my body was warm, so I was forced to run around all the time trying to keep warm. My jacket was made, as we elegantly put it, *of fish fur,* so it provided warmth to the body to this exact extent. The wool, which had been used for my hand-made pullover had a history of trying to keep a few other people warm before me and was used to make many pullovers before mine (and failed!). I was quite proud to wear a pair of woollen and very warm green military trousers sown from a piece of material given to me by one of my friends.

- *Why not to buy a decent Helly Hansen made professional jacket developed specifically for the cold climate?*
- *I am sure that cosmonauts, politicians, Heroes of the Soviet Union and members of the Politburo had access to these commodities, but normal people did not.*

With temperatures as low as -40°C, I could not just stand and wait for a tram warmly packed with people because I was afraid of freezing to death. However, running in the cold had its drawbacks, you know. For example, if you were to run breathing through a scarf to keep as much warmth in your lungs as possible, at some point there would be not enough air and the warm head in the rabbit fur hat would get dizzy. My running speed would depend on the outside temperature, and tended to reduce at lower temperatures. As a rule of thumb, you could judge the temperature and how long you still had to live by trying to spit on the ground - if your saliva hit the ground as a solid it was -45°C and you were in deep trouble. Your feet would be very cold unless you were wearing knee-high boots made of boiled wool, which we called *valenki*, but running in those was utterly impossible. On the bright side, they were good for waiting for a tram, but not for long though.

When, frozen to the depths of your soul, you finally arrived at home, you needed to rub your cheeks and hands and really everything to restore some semblance of blood circulation and carefully deal with those stealthy white spots – signs of frozen and therefore dead tissue.

I half solved the problem with my cold feet by cutting boot inlays from the boiled wool of some old *valenki*, which re-prioritised my hands to the top of the freezing agenda.

- *Did you consider at that time buying warm leather gloves made of inverted fur or good warm synthetic gloves, such as those you might use for skiing?*
- *Come on, such things were not available even in our wildest dreams.*

Unless you were prepared to wear *valenki* on your hands, you were a bit stuck. But even by the more than low fashion standards in Moscow, 1985, wearing *valenki* on your hands would have been regarded as inappropriate, something of a political statement in which case you might have ended up spitting at even lower outside temperatures in some remote part of Russia for the rest of your life. What would you do? I was at my wit's end, and so I did not do much, with my hands getting more and more swollen and red every day through my old woollen mittens because of those damn white spots, which were literally eating my flesh alive.

Then suddenly it was just -20°C outside! It felt like a warm spring, and I was cross-country skiing topless. I was basking in the warmth of the mild winter, my hands were getting better and better every day. It did not matter that I lost a couple of nails, my fingers got through the experience just fine. They are still sensitive to cold weather even today, and one of the first things I bought when I left the USSR was a pair of very warm gloves and mittens. In fact, I still like buying warm gloves and/or receiving them as a present. After all, it is very difficult, and for some people impossible, to get warm after having lived in the USSR.

Do you remember the dialogue between James Bond and Major Amasova in The Spy Who Loved Me?

- *"And what did they teach you at that survival course in Siberia?*
- *Positive mental attitude…"*

In other words, in order to survive you needed to believe not that the winter would soon pass, but that one day you might be able to leave this freezing place…

Now-a-days, for the winter, one can buy very warm mittens, gloves and hats for roughly 1500 roubles (~50 USD) apiece in Moscow, 2011. It is one of the real and indisputable victories of the Perestroika, the democratisation of the Russian society and that innovative development that President Medvedev is constantly talking about. I cannot name any other homemade innovation that immediately springs to mind though… Sorry, another one is the abundance of tea!

These days winters are getting warmer with just the occasional spell of cold weather, otherwise they are pretty dark, gloomy and dull. People occupy visibly more volume in the winter, such that metro trains are packed tight as herrings in a barrel, and it smells like in the cattle yard, as traditionally people prefer wearing fur, leather and leather-inverted jackets.

One thing remains constant – I love mittens and gloves, hats of various kinds, jackets and scarves, socks and pullovers and any kind of warm clothing. I still like receiving and giving presents along these lines. When shopping, I often pop in for a quick look into the sportswear department to update myself, try on or just touch warm jackets and boots and envy the people who wear these sacred garments *in a good way* (as Russians say). At some point, I was seriously considering buying a professional bright-red Helly Hansen winter jacket for polar explorers while I was in Norway… and I still have a warm, cosy dream to have one. I could, but will refrain from writing a ballade about warm boots, I will only say that I would love to turn into butter and slowly melt drop by drop down into those boots!

As Russians used to say (I have not heard any sayings from anyone for a long, long time, so the time of sayings is presumably over): "Steam does not break your bones", or in other words that there is no such thing as being dressed too warm!

Career Pyramid

"Any work here is honourable"

-a popular Soviet slogan-stereotype

I was fond of experimental research when I read Biochemistry in the Medical School. It gave me a feeling of freedom, adventure, intellectual challenge, a new life dimension if you will. It was fun, filled with interesting, old-fashioned and intelligent people, events such as conferences and, importantly, this choice could offer a good, predictable, fairly well paid and potentially respectable career and - who knows – maybe even some foreign travel.

- *Please explain a bit more about that good and predictable career in science.*

- *Ideally, at university in parallel with your studies you would need to do some Komsomol or similar nonsense duties. For example, the Komsomol (a political communist youth organisation) was supposed to serve one purpose – to prepare us for communism, or as Lenin put it, "to learn communism". The problem was that no one understood what communism was or how a sane individual could be prepared for it. Therefore, the Komsomol was vigorously imitating visible activity in this direction by organising various meetings, congresses, seminars...*

- *You got carried away by the Komsomol nonsense as you call it. Please continue telling us how one could make a career in science.*

- *You are right. Now, after graduating, you would need to do a PhD, and this was the most difficult part for obvious reasons. After that, you would become a scientist and then a senior scientist with a salary of up to three hundred roubles, which was twice as much as*

> *that of a practising physician. All posts were permanent, so you would not have to worry about your job security. Whilst a scientific career may not have been not as prestigious as a diplomatic post, and not as desired as a shop manager position, it was definitely more respectable, exciting and quiet than either of THEM.*

- *There seemed to be a unique job hierarchy in the USSR, with medical doctors being paid less than scientists and a diplomatic career being prestigious but not respected. Please could you explain a bit more about what it meant to have a prestigious job?*

I need to explain an interesting psychological perception of a prestigious job in the Soviet Union. There was a granite, some say, hereditary, career pyramid. The most prestigious job was the one that offered an unlimited possibility to travel abroad to capitalist countries, such as a diplomat, a musician, a cosmonaut, an export trade official – I think that covers most of them.

- *You keep talking about this possibility of foreign travel. Why was this parameter of being able to travel abroad so important?*

- *It was important for three reasons. One, because there was no realistic chance to travel abroad other than through work. Second, because this allowed one to acquire things and food of better quality, and third, one could get things from the West and make a good profit by selling or exchanging THEM back home.*

I will give you just one example about someone I personally know. This person brought back an American VCR in the early 1980s with some home-recorded American movies. As you would imagine, this VCR was not new, as it was exploited extremely vigorously on both sides of the Iron Curtain. Then this person decided to sell the VCR along with all the tapes to a man from Georgia (part of the Soviet Union at the time) and got 15,000 roubles for it, which was equivalent to ten years' average salary.

- *What could you actually buy for this amount of money in Moscow in the 1980s?*

- *You could buy outright a two-bedroom apartment in a good district of Moscow and completely furnish it! The person I was referring to has actually bought a cottage near Moscow, which at today's prices is worth around three hundred thousand USD.*

As you can see, it made sense to travel as part of your job, and all Soviet people realised that. There is a higher education institution called the *Moscow Institute of International Relations, MIMO*[99] specialising in training future diplomats, specialists in foreign trade etc, which exactly matched the description of the most prestigious job. However, you would not be able to get in there unless you were born in the right bed, or you fell into the tiny quota for officer veterans of the revolt on the Ochakov cruiser[100]. This joke about the Ochakov revolt refers to some privileges frequently made available in the USSR for non-existent people. Whilst there was no such joke explicitly about MIMO, there were similar ones about many aspects of life in Moscow in the 1980s. For example, there were categories of citizens that could buy food without queues, such as WWII veterans, of which there were not very many left by that time. Therefore, we used to joke that something was available only for the *Veterans of the Shipka Pass battle, 1877*[101], i.e. for people who were no longer alive. In other words, MIMO did not exist for normal people.

You can imagine that these privileged people blessed with the possibility of foreign travel were heartily welcomed and eagerly awaited behind a lot of doors otherwise closed to the general public, such as the Bolshoi Theatre[102], quality food distributors, the specialised retail chain selling foreign goods called Beryozka[103], subsidised district communist party Council canteens, car repair services, box offices of the 'Week of French movies' events, art exhibitions, book shops – you name it. We used to say about these people *Everything around here belongs to the Kolkhoz*[104]*, so everything belongs to me!*. In the public eye, diplomats and foreign trade officials belonged to THEM, and this made these jobs not respectable.

In fact, if we ignore this top level, these was still a possibility to travel abroad at the second level covering the civil service, Ministry officials, some scientists with good connections (we say those supported by *hairy arms*), medical professionals working for THEM in specialised surgeries, clinics, hospitals etc, etc. There were other less interesting business opportunities to travel to countries in Africa and Asia with pro-Soviet regimes if you were a scientist studying, say, dead body preservation, as there were/still are a few dead comrades in mausoleums all over the world.

As for non-business trips, you were allowed to go to a socialist country once every 2 years and to a capitalist country once every five years as a tourist or by an invitation only under strictly regulated conditions.

- *Can you explain, why so?*
- *I guess this is how long on average the understandable culture and consumer shock was supposed to last after visiting a socialist or, even more so, a capitalist country. Trust me, they know a lot about shocks of various types.*

The difference between the first and second levels of foreign travel related jobs was that in the early 1980s the first-level people were not accompanied by a KGB officer whilst abroad. People belonging to all other levels were tightly chaperoned, which I understand was not very pleasant. Perhaps this distinction was an even clearer indication that people employed at the first level did actually belong to THEM.

The rest of the nation could not travel abroad at all. Other criteria of what made a job prestigious had also developed, such as how close you were to the feeding trough (we actually called this *the trough*). Therefore, shop assistants, managers and administrators of stores selling footwear, food (particularly butchers), cosmetics and garments belonged to the next most privileged elite circle. The bottom of the pyramid was left for scientists, engineers, teachers and doctors with unlimited working hours, on-call hours, home visits, miserable salaries – all this balanced against huge responsibilities and duties. As a reflection of the never-changing policy towards professionals, these people were usually referred to in movies, satirical shows, radio performances as feeble intellectuals, someone with a hat on, someone wearing spectacles. One of the best examples of the contrast between different circles within society was given in a well-known performance by the satirical comedian A. Raikin[105] about the deficit of consumer products in the USSR, and what would happen if this situation suddenly disappeared.

- *And just imagine...(pause)... the senior manager... (pause)... of the footwear department!!!...(pause)... sitting (in a theatre) like an ordinary engineer!*

Building a communist society was an interesting experiment. THEM invested a lot of effort to building a highly structured and well-controlled pyramid-like totalitarian edifice, based on fictional values and parameters. Whatever it was, the whole thing was constructed in blatant violation of the elementary laws of physics, and one nice day it just collapsed!

Going into politics or the civil service are at the highest level of the career pyramid in Moscow, 2011. For example, a news story on 27/10/2010 stated that a group of swindlers (or not, who knows?) were arrested for offering a guaranteed post in Moscow or Federal administration for a mere three million US dollars, and they found quite a few clients!

According to Rossiyskaya Gazeta[106], the number of civil servants in Russia over 2005-2006 increased by one hundred and forty-three thousand people (i.e. ~ten percent). The official statistics for 2006 unveiled 1.46 million civil servants (approximately 1% of the general population in Russia; this figure in the USA is 0.7%) not including federal executive bodies dealing with defence and security. Out of all these people, fifty-two and a half percent are employed in the Central apparatus of power.

The civil service in Russia is linked with high job security, a good pension, dental plan and other perks. In addition, each post presents an imaginary barrier to the average citizen, crossing which brings in extra money for the civil servant. I liked the following metaphor, which I heard in a talk show Sparring ('Поединок') in October 2010. If you are a governor or a city mayor, you will control all business and land in this particular fief, and the examples featuring Moscow district prefects and former Moscow mayor Mr. Luzhkov support this notion. The bigger the post, the larger the patrimony land and the more expensive is it to cross the barrier. In a way, the slave-owning society characteristic of the Soviet Union was replaced with a feudal society after 1990, with a clear presence of lordships that own the land, workmanship and vassals, and rule according to their law within their fiefs. It could be that the 'democratisation' phase, which occurred in Russia after 1990, was necessary to subdivide the Russian country into fiefs.

The situation with scientists, doctors and teachers has not changed much, as they are expected not to think about how much money they are earning, but should instead be preoccupied with their noble duty of serving the sovereign[107]. Going abroad after receiving higher education remains a popular decision, particularly among young men, as otherwise they face being drafted into military service for a year, which often results in the loss of their health or life[108]. Pursuing a career not connected to politics, the civil service or business is considered dim-witted, as there are only limited opportunities to progress and/or make money.

American business executives who participated in a meeting with President Medvedev on 11 October 2010 concluded that the lack of professionalism, wide-ranging corruption and the dominance of power structures in business remain major Russian problems. For as long as the Russian government for whatever reason is interested in retaining the old Soviet career pyramid and the associated stereotypes, their comments will remain current.

Is the KGB Omnipresent?

- Why are you immigrating to Israel, Rabinovitch?

- There is no meat, no fish, in fact there is nothing left here, but all this was available just twenty years ago…

- You should think carefully what we could do with you for this defamation!

- Great! Now you haven't even got any ammunition left…

-a Soviet joke

This story is not in line with the usual angles on the KGB, which would probably dwell on the genocide of about thirty percent of the Russian population and making the lives of the rest of the population a living hell. It is not about the official, secret, and probably even super-secret structure of the KGB. It is instead about how it felt to grow up around to this state within a state structure, with its own autonomous medical, education, research, transport, distribution and all kinds of other systems.

Even though pronouncing the name KGB was not a good idea at the time, we all knew it was here, there and everywhere, but you could not touch, hear or see it. It was invisible, but if you talked to anyone, you had to keep a few simple things in mind: one, he or she could be a KGB officer, agent, and informant or just another eager patriotic citizen dreaming to become one; two, you could be eavesdropped on and/or secretly observed absolutely anywhere, even in the middle of a desert. Many of us had relatives and/or friends working for the KGB and frequently were not aware of that fact. I remember one of my father's friends who worked in a supposedly secret KGB department, which dealt with falsifying tourist maps… I was fond of hiking at the time and he advised us against buying any maps, as they were useless. Instead, tourists would use a system of self-made maps and landmarks, which were copied or made by risk loving pioneers. Distributing those maps was a criminal offence.

Let us carry on with geography. The KGB headquarters was strategically located in the heart of Moscow. Potential invaders should take the Kremlin first, and only then only have a five minute drive up the hill along the broad and straight Teatralny Proezd, such that according to military tactics the marching troops would be subjected to fire from the monumental fortress ahead, if indeed those enemy troops are considered to be the enemy. You do not need to guess twice – this building was the KGB headquarters!

It is understood that it was not permitted to take photographs near this infamous building, which encompasses one of the most notorious prisons in Russia. Once, my friends took some pictures of the foreign cars parked next to it. There were no foreign cars elsewhere in the city and we had an understandable interest in the subject. My friends were captured, detained, questioned and their cameras and films were confiscated by people who 'appeared from nowhere' – this was how my friends described the incident. Indeed, thinking about this building, I am sure that the KGB headquarters has windows, or at least something that looks like windows, but no doors, at least none that I can remember. In any case, I cannot recall a single instance of someone entering or leaving this building. Did they seep in through the walls or flush up through secret underground passages?

There is another huge building immediately to its right – the city's biggest kids' department store 'Children's World'. Another huge building, the 'Polytechnic Museum', is located to its left. This museum was particularly famous during 'Khrushchev's thaw' in the early 1960s, when new writers and poets would hold their 'free' speeches within two steps of the most notorious prison and the KGB. Probably this particular neighbourhood created the secure environment for the KGB headquarters. Maybe they had some professional interest in both demographics, children and intellectuals, I mean. In any case, they did have a secret (of course) anti-dissident department No. 5, so maybe they had a similar department against children, too?

- *Where else could not you take photographs in Moscow?*
- *Certainly, not in the metro (which is still the case in 2011)[109]. Not on bridges, at railway stations, airports... If you did not look like a foreign tourist, taking photos would attract real or hidden attention, as indeed any unusual activity did.*

The best way to illustrate the last point is with a story that happened to a couple of friends of mine. By coincidence, both of them had identical briefcases and decided to test the level of alertness and vigilance of the KGB's general surveillance. As part of their experiment, they would both be reading the paper at a newspaper stand which was mounted opposite the restaurant Peking in the city centre, and then pick up the wrong briefcase as if by mistake. Both of them were caught after the third round of this rather stupid game. Your skin colour, the slightest accent or even dialect (Muscovites have a distinct dialect), unusual shoes, ties, jackets, haircut, spectacles, even an overly happy facial expression would attract attention. I was absolutely flabbergasted by someone's remark as I was trying to get onto a tram:

- *Hey, you with the red cheeks, hurry up!*

The point of this anecdote being that there was no way that this man could have seen my face from the back, as it was winter and I was wearing a hat with earflaps, which completely covered my face! As you can see, people in Moscow, 1985 were always watching and many, many of them did not leave these observations for their memoirs. They would go to the KGB reception, which is open twenty-four hours a day and seven days a week, and share their deep thoughts with polite, sporty, well-educated, professionally friendly and caring young men with good manners and the touch of a well-trained smile on their pleasant but easily forgettable faces (does this sound like someone you know?). This is an imaginary report that I think the alcoholic from our filthy communal flat could have delivered gloatingly to a KGB officer in a hope to get our room.

- *I work very hard as a welder in the trolleybus depot welding old buses apart into small pieces, and I have a family with three beautiful innocent children. There is a very strange and potentially dangerous family living in our communal flat. Instead of swearing, beating his wife and drinking stinky and cheap port and all-purpose cleaner all the time as me and all my respectable friends do, he goes to some kind of language course. I am keen to report this highly suspicious behaviour, but I do not have enough money or time to go to the KGB building to discharge my honourable patriotic duty, and maybe, just maybe be awarded our neighbours' small room as compensation for me carrying out my patriotic function. What should I do?*

-    *It is very simple, comrade. Go to the HR department at your depot. ALL HR departments have a "special section" – you understand what that means? They will be able to help you. Thank you, comrade, for your vigilance!*

No matter how attentive citizens like the one who asked the red cheeks question above were, how desperate they and all of us were to spot a KGB officer on the street, we would invariably fail – there were no KGB uniforms around, and this presents KGB mystery number two. Should they not be proud to wear a conspicuous uniform with blue stripes (or whatever)? Were not they proud of what they were (and still are) doing for Russia, the people of Russia and other countries all over the world?

The familiar feeling of the KGB (from April 3, 1995 it is called FSB, Federal Security Service) all around you is still present in Moscow, 2011.

Maybe this feeling comes from strange clicks in the phone receiver and/or echo-like sounds during your phone conversation... Maybe these are militia men checking identification near metro stations, airports, railway stations, patrolling streets and platforms... Maybe it is to do with KGB men dominating all political power structures, society organisations, the Administration of the Russian President (two thirds of staff were ex-KGB in 2007[110] and this number was reduced to one half during the current reign). Maybe our memory is refreshed in an orchestrated manner by the mass media after the next botched operation and/or demonstration of power and omnipresence of the KGB, such as the scandal over the alleged spy ring of eleven people in the USA in summer 2010 and the poisoning of Alexander Litvinenko (a former KGB officer who defected to the UK and was poisoned with Polonium-210). Among other things, Litvinenko accused the Kremlin of staging the apartment block bombings in Russia in September 1999, just about half a year before the Presidential Elections in March 2000 that brought Mr. Putin to power on the wave of nationalism and threats from internal and external enemies. Strangely enough, I had exactly the same gut feeling when it happened… It does not make you feel secure if there are reasons to believe that your home can be blasted away if THEM need it for an election campaign.

On the one hand, KGB and militia (soon to be renamed to police) are merging with power structures, and on the other hand, they integrate into the criminal world to control drug trafficking, illegal luxury car business, prostitution and weapons trade. You will hear thousands of stories that militia in Nishniy Tagil controls drug trafficking, that officials from Internal Ministry handle illegal elite car business, that local governors are involved in the illegal export of Russian timber to China on various talk shows on TV and in newspapers. The common perception is that criminal cases are closed, jury members put under pressure and judges manipulated if THEM are found involved in criminal activity of any kind.

The insecurity of people is constantly reinforced on a subconscious level by the dominance of violent movies and TV shows, showing aggressive episodes and dead people in TV news, rude and often cruel TV talk shows and an increased level of vindictiveness around you in the streets and public transport. As a result, levels of overall confusion and tolerance to criminals in general population have increased, such that people just calmly continued swimming and bathing after a speedboat drove over a young lady this summer near Moscow cutting her into pieces (the driver was one of THEM and the case was closed).

I often ask myself why foreign businesses keep coming to Russia. Maybe they are being made offers they can not refuse?

It's off to Work We Go

"They are pretending to pay us salaries, and we are pretending to work"

-a popular joke in the 1980s

I worked in Moscow between my graduation and emigration, from the early 1980s to the early 1990s. In general, whether or not a clock-in system was present at a particular workplace, discipline was strictly enforced, such that arriving a few minutes late or leaving a few minutes early could lead to dismissal or practical conclusions. The visible consequences of practical conclusions would be a collective discussion of the event, then a formal reprimand and after a few repeat occurrences, dismissal for truancy. It definitely did not sound very pleasant, so we tried hard not to be late for work. There would be frequent checks carried out by the most important people at work - Human Resources - in the working area and/or at the entrance check point to ensure compliance with the working discipline. If you were alive and wanted to stay that way, it was a good idea to be working, unless you were ill (supported by a form signed off by a local doctor) or completely loopy.

- *Why were those people from Human Resources the most important?*
- *Because they reported directly to the Director and the KGB, and quite possibly were on the KGB payroll.*

In the 1980s, working discipline was far less strict than during Stalin's rule when those late for work would be prosecuted and sentenced for a period to perform forced unpaid labour at a Gulag. Afterwards, those people would have a note in their labour books[111] and much reduced chance of finding a decent job for the rest of their lives. Therefore, rule number one – whatever happens, be at work!

There were a lot of volunteers recruited by the KGB, which were present in every section, laboratory, working unit. They were called knockers (стукачи) and they discharged honourable duties - to report unofficially (i.e. for free, just for pure pleasure) to the KGB anything remotely suspicious that they heard, seen, observed, witnessed or sometimes just imagined. In addition, of course, there were official knockers who did this professionally, i.e. as a matter of principle, money and career. There was no way to find out who they were, you just needed to stick to rule number two – be careful about what you say to sudden news, say, about a demise of the current Secretary General of the communist party. It would be a mistake to follow my grandmother's example, who used to say about Stalin's death *A dog's death for a dog* (собаке – собачья смерть). If you cannot hide your joy, try to conceal it with sobs and tears, just like Chief Inspector Dreyfus did when he gave a eulogy about the alleged death of Inspector Clouseau in one of the Pink Panther films.

Rule number three was that your boss had absolute power over you, his boss had a similar standing over your boss, with the Director being equivalent to an Emperor if not God Almighty to all of his employees. To illustrate this point, I will cite a popular joke, which was used in one of the many faceless movies about brave KGB men and lawbreakers. One of the latter asked his peer about the position of a particular person in the Soviet hierarchy:

-      *And how high exactly is his position?*
-      *He is positioned so high that you can see Magadan*[112]
       from his office!

Every Director was sitting so high that he could easily show you the direction to Magadan if you happened to forget where it was. For many years when I was exposed to my Director, I could not look into his eyes at all. When I felt particularly brave, I risked raising my eyes at his secretary. He never shouted at people, he did not need to. In the early 1980s, he was an embodiment of power and conviction of the communist ideals, and you could not argue with that. In the late 1980s, when the Perestroika was marching through the country the Director became a democrat and later he stopped mentioning the communist past as if it never existed. I have kept in touch with him for various reasons, and then I discovered that he was just an old man without convictions, beliefs, morals, deep interests, attractions or affections, just like a piece of forgotten plasticine ready to be shaped into something else, and this discovery made me a bit sad and full of pity for him.

Since at work every step and breath were decided for you, there was nothing to worry about if you were wise enough to stick to the above three rules. What was I doing during my time at work (only about 15% of which was filled with actual work) after graduating with a biochemistry diploma? I was drinking tea all the time, tried to learn French with not much success, then got into genealogy, puzzle solving, learning English - because you could not just sit and wait for the next order to be implemented. As we used to say, *Initiative is punishable*, so there was no initiative whatsoever, but plenty of spare time to be filled. We tried each other's cake recipes, had long discussions about movies, books, exhibitions (no politics, as there might have been knockers around), hobbies like growing houseplants (in particular, African violets). After midday, everyone would become vividly interested in where to buy (or *get*) things or food in preparation for The Main Attraction at 1 pm – the lunch break!

Ready, steady, go and within milliseconds, all desks were empty, although the cigarette smoke would stick around for a few minutes. All athletes were rushing through the entrance check-in aiming for grocery stores, second-hand shops and bookshops, department stores, box offices, post offices, dry cleaners, photo studios and countless other places. Albert Einstein was right, if you travel close to the speed of light, time really does slow down. It was amazing what trained people could do in just one hour during the lunch break! The rest of the day would be spent on assessing what other people managed to get during the lunch break. Someone was left at work as a sentinel, and he managed to write a whole book of poetry, someone else passed a driving test, one lady bought a wedding dress for her daughter, who managed to get married and divorced – all in just one hour!

However, what was that? The sentinel-poet was giving the predetermined signal – the people from HR were coming over. In an instant, everyone was back at their stations in a working gown, looking through protective glasses into a particle accelerator, microscope, colorimeter, telescope, discussing the deviation of planets from their paths by dark matter, the behaviour of elementary particles, or just shooting red lasers, transcontinental rockets, satellites (maybe that's how Sputnik-1 was launched?)[113]... We all looked motivated, determined to *catch up with and overtake America*[114], to conquer continents and worlds in the spirit of the communist party ideals.

We used to go to a pub (called Pivnaya or beer house) after work for a glass or two of Shigulevskoye beer – a yellowish watery substance without foam but with some vague beer smell, which we used to call quite rightly urine. The lads would add a bit of vodka or just pure ethanol to the drink which would increase the alcohol content from nearly zero to the desired value. On the bright side though, however hard you tried with this brand of beer you would never become an alcoholic.

Right in the middle of my progression towards the title of the best tea drinker in the world, I decided to do a PhD in Biochemistry. I did this within one (OK, maybe two!) of my lunch breaks. Then I learned English (one more lunch break) and left the plasticine Director in his office with a view, together with the vigilant knockers, the watery Shigulevskoye beer, the never-ending hunting season of the HR people and the entire Centre of Communism altogether.

I was working in science in Moscow, 1985, so I shall continue with science in Moscow, 2011. Russian science is disappearing, such that *Russia has been a leader in scientific research and intellectual thinking across Europe and the world for so long that it comes not only as a surprise but a shock to see that it has a small and dwindling share of world activity as well as real attrition of its core strengths*[115]. Indeed, Russian scientific research accounts for about 2.6% of scientific papers indexed by Thomson Reuters falling behind India (2.9%) and far behind China (8.4%). Russian research institutes have research budgets amounting to three to five percent of comparably sized organisations in the USA, and just one percent of Russians polled in 2006 named science as a prestigious career.

It seems from this data that continuous tea drinking had a profoundly deleterious effect on Russian science and technology, with almost no ongoing research in agriculture and computer science. I visited my friend at the State Research Institute, and the situation has not changed since the time I was working in Russia in the 1980s! Even the most essential equipment is lacking, and, in essence, even active medical scientists work using methods developed and introduced by L. Pasteur[116] in the 19th century! Judging by this particular institute, the solution seems to be in recruiting a new Director with … a military background, increasing discipline, introducing a clock-in system and a guarded entrance, inventarisation of all equipment without replacing the outdated kit… All this sounds very familiar, suggesting that working in science has not changed at all.

The common view is that working in modern Soviet (renamed to Russian) administrative structures including the Prefects of the Moscow regions or the Moscow Mayor is associated with lucrative real estate business within their fiefs. Russians perceive the KGB to be involved in controlling drugs, luxury car business and prostitution, whereas the military is more into weapons and human organ sales extracted from new recruits. Any journalists rocking the boat are usually demonstratively beaten dead or half-dead[117] and then (an interesting twist) often prosecuted and sentenced under various pretences[118]. The new order is supported by the ever-obliging mass media and film directors, with a handful of well-controlled mild dissidents in various areas who are historically allowed to criticise, such as M. Zhvanetsky[119].

The new working culture of Moscow, 2011 is not unanimously accepted by all Russian scientists and specialists alike, such that about 1 million people officially emigrated from the USSR/Russia between 1990-2000, further four hundred and forty thousand people left between 2003-2008[120] mainly to *get some fresh air*, and the current rate is estimated at about three hundred and fifty thousand per year[121]. Taking into account how difficult it is to get a job in the West, we can be safe in assuming that those people were well educated, had foreign language knowledge, were professionals in their field, such as the 2010 Nobel Prize winners in Physics Andre Geim and Konstantin Novoselov who work at Manchester University in the UK[122].

It Was All About Money, Wasn't It?

"Take every nail from the factory – after all, you are the owner, not a guest!"

"Неси с завода каждый гвоздь, ведь ты хозяин, а не гость!"

-Popular joke in the 1980s

As the Secretary-General of the communist party L. I. Brezhnev used to say, there is no problem in distributing goods around the Soviet Union – just get them to the working places and then they will be carried away. Therefore, people who were stealing from work were called carriers (несуны) and everyone was stealing from work at the time, including Brezhnev himself. But how much exactly?

My wife had an old friend from an old Bolshevik family. Once she told me after visiting her friend that there was a very expensive and old concert piano at her house, which had been confiscated from a bourgeois family after the Revolution. This made me very sad at the time, and I am still sad on this account. For some reason, I always imagine pretty children playing this piano with their parents standing behind them and smiling quietly. Suddenly some big people in leather jackets come, shoot the parents and carry away their stuff arguing how to divide the expropriated loot. That old Bolshevik family had some very expensive and old jewellery, too…

The expropriation system was based on confiscating goods from tsarist loyalists, aristocrats, the bourgeoisie and then from the state and finally from other Bolsheviks after their arrests, and this system was at the heart of the Bolshevik domestic trade system. THEM did not do much to destroy it, suggesting that it was somehow beneficial for THEM. I am absolutely convinced that this was a wise tactical move for a number of reasons.

- *I cannot believe what you are saying! What could be good about stealing?*

-    *Many things. One, EVERYONE could be caught and imprisoned because of stealing at any time. This rule still holds. Secondly, it tied THEM together, just as induction rituals involving bloodshed tie together members of criminal gangs. Finally, it removed a psychological barrier concerning the property of other people, it prompted normal people to stick their noses into other people's lives and report if someone had slightly better living standards. It destroyed the morals, responsibility and the guilt normally associated with stealing. If you do not have something, just go and steal it! For example, in summer 2008, I was stunned by a radio report that a visitor to Moscow Zoo liked a chimpanzee so much that he came back in the evening and stole it!*

The practice of stealing was so deeply ingrained in society that no-one saw anything wrong with glamorising stealing in one of the most popular Soviet cartoons for children called Prostokvashino. The uncle of the cat character was working at a shoe-polish factory and kept sending packages with free shoe-polish to all his relatives. Amazingly, it seemed like a reasonable explanation at the time!

Embezzling was happening on two levels. At the level of normal people, it was governed by the Act of the Council of Peoples' Commissaries of 7 August 1932 on the Protection of Socialist Property, according to which public property was declared the cornerstone of the Soviet regime. All those encroaching on Socialist possessions were automatically considered enemies of the state, and these crimes qualified as state crimes involving ten years' imprisonment in a gulag and confiscation of all personal property. From then on, there was never a problem for the Soviet Union to have as many slaves as they wanted, as the labour camps were constantly replenished with people guilty of stealing a loaf of bread, some ears of corn or even tailings from a Kolkhoz field, a rotten bolt from a factory dumping ground… This law applied to criminals from the age of twelve[123].

Therefore, embezzling at this first level was difficult and dangerous, where particular methods of stealing were deemed acceptable for only particular places of work. For example, in the mid-1980s, I tried to earn a few extra roubles working at a meat distribution centre in Moscow for several nights a week, where we loaded and unloaded huge refrigerator containers filled with all kinds of meat. At lunch breaks at about 1:00 am, we could eat as much meat as we wanted, but we could not take a gram of it with us. Over lunch, the workers would share their experiences of how to pass the checkpoint, with the easiest advice being to tape it around one's legs.

The second level of embezzling was at the party and state levels; however, this time with no restricting laws at all.

- *Could you make a rough estimate of the scale of this embezzlement?*

- *I can certainly try, using open sources of information about the last few years of the Soviet regime. For obvious reasons, there is no information on the current situation.*

It is now well known that the communist party possessed its own shadow economy, gold reserves and investment policy. Several criminal cases were opened and secret documents became available in the late 1980s before the dissolution of the communist party that gave an idea of the scale of this high-level embezzlement:

- The criminal case N18/6220-91 On the investigation of financial and economic activities of the CPSU Central Committee attracts our attention to the funds that were often allocated to friends of the CPSU, amounting to approximately 0.8 billion dollars[124];

- On 21 June 1989, State Customs removed all restrictions on gold transfers from Russia, which resulted in the reduction of the Russian gold reserves from 2500 tonnes in 1985 to about 250 tonnes in 1991; all gold produced during this time (around 1500 tonnes) obviously disappeared as well[125];

- Acquiring land, property, banks and industry in Russia. The small and medium-sized companies alone that were established in the late 1980s and owned by the party were estimated to be worth five billion dollars;

- Money laundering involving foreign credits of about 144 billion dollars;

- Transfers of highly insecure funds of the new bourgeois class, consisting mainly of former party Apparatchiks and Nomenclature, estimated to be between 150-268 billion dollars alone in 1992-1999.

Just in the last decade before new millennium, THEM worked very hard and were rewarded with at least five hundred and twenty-three billion dollars, not taking into account the last and most valuable source of money – gas and oil! Nothing suggests that THEM were doing something that THEM had not done before, such that we can easily assume that THEM were earning roughly 0.5 trillion dollars every decade, and probably accumulated on their savings accounts about four trillion dollars...

-    *Are you actually suggesting that communism was in fact all about money?*
-    *Surely that is a rhetorical question.*

In the mid-1980s, I had no money but we had to prepare homemade cottage cheese for my little son every day. Therefore, I was stealing milk from work, too.

There are examples in this book that suggest that communism, all these Great Revolutions and words about patriotism, and in fact, <u>everything</u> about THEM was merely about extra pocket money. This extra cash by definition could not be stored in Russia, so the scale of capital outflows to the West is one good indicator of their appetite in Moscow, 2011.

According to the Round table of business in Russia[126], a new wave of capital outflows started in the late 1980s and by the mid 1990s the total volume of overseas resources amounted to about 600 billion US dollars, i.e. about 70 billion US dollars per year. This tendency seems to be stable, as during January-March 2010 Russia lost about thirteen billion US dollars (it lost 21.3 billion US dollars during the same three months in 2011[127]) to the illegal capital transfer (i.e. about 50 billion US dollars projected loss in 2010, which is about twenty-five percent of the annual state revenue[128]). That sounds about right...

As everything including all big and medium-sized business belongs to THEM, so the channels and the extent of embezzling are obvious - a quarter or the entire annual Russian annual budget revenue goes abroad plus probably another quarter consumed internally! This means that each Russian is robbed by about 1,000 US dollars per year.

A Cossack Village

Live your lives, brothers, while Moscow doesn't notice you, because once it does, it won't let you live.

(Живите, братцы, пока Москва не видит, Москва увидит, жить не даст)

-a visionary Cossack saying of the pre-Soviet era

My brother and I spent a few hot summers in the mid-1980s in the torrid south-western regions of Russia traditionally populated by Cossacks[129]. I liked them, their strong survival instinct and their traditional way of life or whatever was left of it after the Red Wheel[130] rolled over them. We went to one particular household to scythe grass, as well as to cut down and chop firewood in exchange for food and a roof over our heads. It is not important how we came up with this idea, but it worked and we enjoyed ourselves immensely.

The village was about five to six hours' walking distance from the nearest train station, with an invisible path going along a small river rarely coinciding with a dirt road, which was doing bizarre zigzags from the river to the hills about ten km away. Because of the extreme heat, it was impossible to get to the village in one day. It was a good excuse for us to stay overnight in a tent on a river bank, make a campfire and brew Cossack tea made with thyme and oregano, warm up some plain food, setting off for the village early in the morning. The village was shrinking every summer, with more and more houses becoming deserted, empty and gazing sadly with their glassless windows at our noisy arrival to meet Pyotr Stepanovitch - a former blacksmith and Head of the Kolkhoz. Pyotr Stepanovitch was in his 80s, but I would not dare compete with him in cutting down, chopping wood, handling haystacks or sharpening knives. He was also unbeatable at disputing philosophical questions. Just like the extremely fertile black soil around, he seemed to have scrutinised his life experience in a most productive and positive way. He did not tell us anything about life that we did not already know, but the way he put it was a revelation. I remember asking him:

- Pyotr Stepanovitch, you said that your dad was killed by Bolsheviks. How did it happen?

- Well, pretty much in the same way as they killed most of the villagers. They did not even bother to bury THEM, they just gathered THEM up, escorted THEM to the river and then shot THEM all dead"[131].

There was no pain or protest in his voice. I was under the impression that I was given a rare chance to talk to someone from beyond this world, to get a glimpse at the ultimate human wisdom and acceptance of the world around us. I have had this type of an existentialist experience just a handful of times in my life, the other times with an ex-Nazi concentration camp prisoner (he lived in the same communal flat as my family) and ex-White movement officer (he was my relative who fled from Russia after the Civil war and lived in Paris, France ever since)…

- *Can you remember anything else about that unique man?*

- *He did not talk much. I also remember the movements of his hands when he sharpened my knife that I tried to use for woodcarving. He probably was not even physically sharpening it – he was endowing it with sharpness. I remember his posture and gestures, which were very similar to the body language of English nobility, as it turned out to be.*

I also remember his story about how he treated himself for spinal rheumatism when he was in his 50s. He could barely move by that time, and someone helped him to the sandy riverbanks. Pyotr Stepanovitch buried himself in the hot sand for a day, leaving just his head above the ground, after which the pain was gone forever! I should point out that even touching this sand in the summer could easily burn your fingers, let alone burying your whole body in it!

Once I had a chance to talk to his grandson who was about my age at the time. He wanted to buy a machinegun and go to the

Red Square to shoot as many of THEM as possible. We were drinking, shouting and coming up with arguments for and against this idea, and Pyotr Stepanovitch was looking at us with a quiet smile on his lips. I honestly do not know whether his grandson ever did this – he could well have done, as he was a Cossack after all!

It was great to get up very early in the morning with the dew still fresh on the grass, walk to the remote meadow patches designated for private hay production and then scythe the grass until lunch. Unlike my brother, I was not very good at it at all, but I became a professional hay-stacker instead. After that, we would swim in the small crystal-clear river and lie in the shadow of a weeping willow on the yellow sand that healed our bodies and souls from the hard work. There was nothing to remind you of the bloody year of 1919 when almost the entire village was massacred by an NKVD (former name of KGB) patrol squadron, with corpses blocking the river flow and red sand covering the river banks all the way down to its confluence with the river Don.

We were a bit sick of eating bread and potatoes all the time, and one day we decided to pick some wild mushrooms to fry or make into a soup. The forests around the village were full of them, but the locals did not pick them at all. We had a nice walk and collected a few wild mushrooms, but left one king of a mushroom that I found at the edge of the forest. It was so unusually big, beautiful and noble that I just could not take it. We were about to start peeling and washing the mushrooms for our wild mushroom risotto, as Pyotr Stepanovitch told us that the locals do not pick mushrooms for a reason. Back in 1919, THEM had separated the Ataman and all the children from the rest of the villagers, and apparently shot them dead in those forests. Since that time, that beautiful stately mushroom has been growing in that spot, where the Ataman was decapitated with a cavalry sword... To this day, I am sometimes put off eating mushrooms by this memory.

Their last directive - which terminated the agony of the Cossacks, their unique civilisation and way of life, philosophy, complex society structure, spirit of freedom and patriotism – was in the form of a telegram with just eight words, which to me epitomise the whole Marxism-Leninism philosophy. It was sent by Lenin to the Cheka (former name of the KGB) head Felix

Dzerzhinsky on 19 December 1919 with a clear order with regard to the one million Cossacks held prisoner in the Cheka camps: to kill each and every one of THEM.

The gloomy prediction of the Cossacks cited in the beginning of this story turned out to be true, THEM finally noticed and exterminated the Cossacks in 1919. THEM were in essence just a very efficient killing machine that targeted everything alien to THEM, which, let us face it, was pretty much everything. Let us just pray that THEM will not notice the rest of the planet in the same way…

The Cossacks are back, so it seems at least. Indeed, seven million people consider themselves Cossacks in 2010. About twenty Cossack voiskos (regiments) have been restored, and the Cossacks were finally recognised as a distinct ethno-cultural entity and military force by a bill On the State Service of Russian Cossacks endorsed by The State Duma[132] on 18 May 2005. It appears that there is nothing to worry about. I have a strange question – are these the same Cossacks?

There is a tiny difference between the new and old Cossacks, which is the carefully modified credo, which used to be For Faith, the Tsar and Fatherland, transformed into For Faith, Liberty and Fatherland. What if were to transform the credo of the French Revolution Liberté, Égalité, Fraternité (Liberty, Equality, Fraternity) into something else? Would it still be the same French Revolution?

Cossacks, look into your hearts – you are a rare living example of a people who had the honour and privilege of swearing allegiance to the Russian Tsar and to the Orthodox Autocracy in general, and not to a mysterious Liberty, which has never been present in Russia. The Orthodox faith, loyalty to the Russian Tsar and our Fatherland were the core principles of your civilisation. To the Orthodox believers the Russian monarch, and not liberty, is second after God! THEM have replaced just a single word in your oath, and all Cossacks along with all Russians have been enslaved by local and central criminal authorities, exemplified by the situation around Cossack village (staniza) Kushevskaya[133] (a village of Black Sea Cossacks located on the river Eya between the city of Krasnodar and Rostov-na-Donu in the Krasnodar region). The population of ~thirty thousand people has been practically enslaved by criminal gangs supported by local militia, administration and KGB (FSB) for the last twenty years. During this time, about two hundred cases of rape and three hundred murders were registered, and all these cases were closed. Upon interference by the local newspaper, a grenade was detonated in the newspaper office. Complaints to the central power structures were futile. The situation culminated on 4-5 November 2010, when twelve people in a house (including four children, the youngest one just nine months old) were brutally massacred by four gangsters. The victims had at least three knife wounds each, and the youngest child was killed by one of the killers holding his foot on the child's throat.

Cossacks have been noticed in Moscow, 2011. According to the new legislation on Cossacks proposed by the President Medvedev of 19.02.2011, the Chief Cossack (Ataman) will be appointed by the President from now on, and not elected as it used to be the case[134].

Shabashka Friends

"Shabashka: time free from work (archaic)"

- Ushakov's Explanatory Dictionary

Shabashka (summer 'cash-in-hand' work), a seasonal construction business of temporary labour collectives in the USSR in the 1980s, where collective and state farms could spend cash on the construction of certain small-scale facilities, such as schools, fences, houses, farms etc. Payment for this work was done in cash which attracted seasonal workers of various professional and educational backgrounds, particularly during summer time. On average those seasonal workers, such as scientists and engineers, would earn for their hard labour during their holidays around 1000 roubles per month, which was equivalent to about eight months of their day-job salary.

In the mid-1980s, the Soviet government upgraded the state food distribution policy by introducing 'food orders' or 'food hampers' usually distributed via canteens at work. One of the clear advantages was that ordinary people would spend less time looking for food during their lunch breaks.

I had three quite materialistic problems and there was no way how I could have solved them unless I went to shabashka with my friends. First, I was very cold in my fish fur jacket in the winter and, understandably, I wanted to have a warm coat to wear. Second, our freezer compartment was too small to accommodate frozen fruit, vegetables and meat, which suddenly materialised from nowhere at my work canteen[135], so we needed a proper freezer. Finally, I felt the quality of our life could improve greatly if we had a sewing machine, which would have opened many possibilities. I reckoned I would need about nine hundred to one thousand roubles to buy all this treasure. No, there were no such things as deferred payment plans or interest-free loans; you had to buy everything upfront.

A friend of mine, Mikhail, a physicist (now a USD multi-millionaire), made all the necessary arrangements, including our travel permit to the border of the USSR, with his relative who was heading up a collective farm in the northern part of Russia. Mikhail therefore became our informal chief and taskmaster. As it was usually the case with shabashka workers, all five of us had university degrees and we all were working on our PhDs in Medicine, Biochemistry, Physics, Elementary Particles and something to do with the military application of lasers. The laser guy Dima did not talk too much about this stuff (I cannot blame him because otherwise he would have gone straight to a gulag), but he was clearly a very important acquisition for our shabashka commune, as he worked as a qualified welder. I took with me a very thick and heavy Biochemistry manual to read and pure ethanol (which I got through my unnamed Biochemistry channels) for undisclosed purposes, as this story happened bang in the middle of Gorbachev's campaign against vodka[136].

- *I can accept the need for ethanol, but it is not at all obvious why you would bother taking a heavy Biochemistry manual when embarking on such a trip?*
- *You are right; of course, I had no time to read it. Nevertheless, it was heavy and once it came in handy when the Elementary Particles guy Andrey got a cold. We wrapped him in a mustard bandage and used my book to press the warm bandage tightly against his chest. He was fit as a fiddle in no time.*

The medicine man Ivan (we called him Doc) was a gynaecologist, not really something that one would immediately need in a boys' shabashka club, but he knew enough about general practice medicine as well. He was quite fussy about his hands at the start, saying he could not afford to damage them (strange guy), but by the end of the enterprise, he could bend thick nails with just three fingers. Andrey and I were useless in terms of actual building work, we could not lay bricks as well as Mikhail or compete with Ivan on the plumbing side, and so what we did was to hand mix concrete for the entire four weeks. It was fun. When I raised my head out of the concrete mixing bath every so often, I was usually dazed with daylight and strange flashes of light sparkled in front of my eyes. In those precious moments, I would enjoy the view of a lake and dream that one day I might come closer to seeing it. Sometimes I would notice a similar crazy expression in Andrey's eyes on the other side of the bath, which was amplified by the fact that we both avoided wearing our spectacles as these could have easily fallen into the concrete.

I remember dragging my feet to a public Russian sauna (banya) for a weekly wash. It was Sunday, the only day we would allow ourselves to get some rest after the previous 6 working days each filled with twelve+ hours' hard labour. After entertaining myself in front of the concrete bath for the last three weeks, I was too weak to soap myself in one go, so I had to break down this enormous task into lots of small steps. Luckily, there was only half of my bodyweight and probably volume left, the rest was lost together with the sweat in the concrete bath. I was exhausted to the point that I slept without undressing myself, just like Neznaika[137], and I felt that Andrey would follow suit very soon, he must have had more elementary particles inside his body than me.

Doc figured that working so hard was somehow stressful for our bodies, so he gave us a bit of diluted ethanol every day equivalent to about one hundred ml of vodka. We called this daily stress relief mixture "our military one hundred grams" by analogy with the same practice in the Soviet Army during WWII[138]. Then we started to have problems with the skin on our swollen fingers, it simply did not want to stay there anymore, it was cracking and trying to come off, and again Doc was there for us, this time with his tinctures and creams. Maybe we were just shedding our old skin and shells like snakes and crabs do when they grow out of their old shape.

- *Did you have fun during this time at all?*
- *I remember once our chief Mikhail went to his relative's for a party or something. His absence relaxed our limits in terms of our military one hundred grammes and we had a bit more and then a bit more. Then we were invited by the locals to play volleyball, and it was really fun. Neither Andrey nor I could see the ball without our glasses anyway, so we were playing regardless of the actual location of the ball. I assume that Dima and Doc*

acted like true professionals, just like at the building site. It sounds amazing but we actually won the game. I remember this volleyball game now with warmth and gratitude.

By the hardest fourth week, I was so exhausted that I could fall asleep at any moment, as if bitten by a tsetse fly[139]. During our rare breaks, I would fall asleep with a spade in my arms and my head down the familiar concrete mixing bath. Probably if I had fallen down at that moment into the concrete and been left there for a while, I would have become a monument to the Shabashka movement. When I started to go to bed wearing my cement-hard clothes after work, I realised that I should either leave or die. It happened after nearly four weeks of the hardest labour I could have ever imagined in my wildest dreams. I left together with Dima, as the building site had run of things to be cemented or welded. When I got to the train, I slept like a dead man, on my back and completely motionless on a plain wooden berth without a mattress or pillow for about twenty-four hours, lulled by the familiar flashes of light and the view of the mysterious lake that I never got a chance to see up close.

During that summer, I got nearly 900 roubles, and we bought a warm coat, a sewing machine and a freezer.

Evidently, Shabashka did not kill me, but contrary to common belief, nor did it make me stronger. However, it helped me shed the old skin together with illusions that there was a helping hand out there for me, that things would ever get better, or that I could ever fit in. Most importantly, the large freezer bought with the shabashka money provided us with frozen vitamins and proteins to last those endless winters that remained until our eventual departure from Moscow.

In just 25 years time after our shabashka, Andrey became a computer programmer and lives in Knoxville, TN; Doc is now a great gynaecologist, other shabashka friends went into business and became more or less wealthy.

When we see each other every year in Moscow, the first toast is always to Dima who died in a car crash together with his daughter and father in 1997.

Going West

"Baby eagles are learning to fly..."

-a popular Young Pioneer song

Young Pioneers are in this context not those who colonised the American West, but the official name for a political organisation in the USSR for children between the ages of nine and fourteen. The organisation was founded in 1922 by analogy to the Scout movement in the West, but very quickly it became a political structure.

I am sure there is a gene that contains the code for a protein that does not stick to anything, it has no charge, it cannot be handled, purified or cloned (otherwise this gene would be known already, wouldn't it?). This gene makes people wanderers who cannot stick to anything. If you are suppressed, for instance during the communist rule, the gene is frequently over-expressed, and then people will dig holes in concrete with their bare hands or they just die.

I was probably about ten years old when I decided that I wanted to leave. Maybe it happened straight after birth, maybe even before, during the antenatal period. In other words, for as long as I remember myself and to the deepest depths of my soul and heart I always wanted to go. And if I had two or more souls I would take care to take all of them with me, I would not leave one behind just to see what would happen, I knew what would happen just too well. I had no more questions to ask of this place.

I had just done my PhD and undergone a rigorous English course. It was not that I was preparing to leave, as you could not possibly leave Moscow, 1985. The concrete wall was tough, tall and absolutely impenetrable. I just managed to scratch the surface. I was wandering through Moscow and I just could not accept that there was no way I could possibly leave.

THEM were having a war in Afghanistan, do not ask me why (there is something there that makes all countries greedy and bloodthirsty, too bad for the Afghan people, as you cannot kill the entire nation which would have been the only way to win this war). I seriously began to consider volunteering for this war with a view to be killed not to kill. Luckily, someone mentioned to me that there was a guy who had just returned from the USA[140]. Apparently, he wanted to do another scientific degree (Doctor of Sciences, DSc) to get a better job back in the USA? How bizarre...

I arranged a meeting with him and began to feel small pieces of concrete wall on my hands...

- *"You just write your job applications to the labs that do similar research. I will give you my CV as an example, and voila. Write as many as you can and in a year, you will have a job offer."*

That was his advice.

This is the precipitated wisdom from this meeting. Instead of my bare hands, I suddenly felt I had a bulldozer behind me and so I was acting like one. The list of one hundred or so addresses was made in an instant, and I was quickly writing my first applications and printing copies of my CV on my dad's computer. I decided to send at least four applications per week to go through the list in half a year. I could not use a photocopier, as those were not available. I will tell you a secret – photocopiers were very, very treacherous things, as they could be used to copy prohibited literature.

- *Why are you showing the return address on all these letters? – asked a friendly post office clerk.*
- *???*
- *You do not want* THEM *to come for you, do you?*

It was in 1989 and the times of the Inquisition were over. I did not care anymore. I was writing those letters, and the hole was opening up reluctantly. I cannot remember much from that year - my son was growing, the seasons apparently were changing, I was going to work and even made some kind of a career in science. What I remember is the total sense of absorption and devotion to the cause of drilling. There was no pain, no tiredness, no hesitation, no mercy, and no hunger; there were no feelings at all and I was sitting on a powder keg all the time. The task was clear, the stake was my life.

Together with the frozen postman who must have descended from the heavens, I was gazing before long at a letter from the USA, which had come in an envelope with an imprinted Eagle. I have never seen this mysterious postman either before or after this event, who was he? An angel? A secret agent? I could not possibly open the letter, I was staring at it as a sheep at a new gate (Russian saying). It was real and it was not. The smell was different, and so was the taste. I did not know what I was supposed to do with it. I left the opening ceremony until the evening meal.

- *I got a letter from the USA by registered post today.*
- *So what? –* (you cannot impress your wife, whatever you do, ever).
- *What did it say? –*(the key question always comes from children).
- *I do not know. I have not opened it. I am scared.*
- *I can open this letter for you –* (you can always rely on your children).

It was from the National Institute of Health, Bethesda, MD, and it was serious, but not serious enough for me go pack my suitcase. I gave myself my word that I would go for the first serious interview offer, which came a couple of months, a few grey hairs and wrinkles later from the Max-Planck Institute in West Berlin, Germany. Now thinking about it, all this must have happened in 1989 BC, too much has happened since, too much water has flowed away.

I still have the same dream from time to time. I am flying over a city, then I see a wall, and suddenly I just fly over it. And I always ask myself in this dream: How come it's so easy?'

It was not so easy after all, but in my view this is fair enough. All who tread through the same path know that if you are from Russia you have to be ten times better (and/or work ten times harder) than an average local or European applicant for the same job to be offered one. I had a look at the Manchester University webpage on Konstantin Novoselov (Nobel Prize laureate in

Physics, 2010) on 29 November 2010, and his position was listed as Research Associate (the entry level of PhD graduates in research at a British university). Even if you get a Nobel Prize, you are still at the bottom of the pyramid.

For the first six or seven years, you are a slave because your immigration status falls into that category. If you work for less than twelve hours a day, sleep for longer than five hours a day and on top of that also enjoy spending weekends with your family, you will lose both your job and your place in the country in a second. I was writing countless grants and papers, and the accolade, money and prestige went to the leading Reader who then became a Professor. It was equitable to the interests of both parties though, as in return, I was able to sort out my immigration status, and we are not slaves anymore. It might be fun to write a separate book about that.

A. P. Chekhov said that all his life he was trying to squeeze the slave out of him. He did not mention that it was impossible to do it in Russia and that even if you leave, you will only find another concrete wall ahead of you that you need to drill through to become free.

Life-String

"One cannot manage without his fatherland, but the fatherland can manage without any one of us"

-Joseph Stalin

I wrote this allegory in 1984. The original Russian text was lost, and it was better not to keep such texts in any event. I am reproducing this text in English from my memory with some modifications. I thought I should include this short story, as it represents the way I genuinely felt about life in the USSR at the time, which could be of interest to the reader from a psychological point of view.

Once upon a time, there was a young man living in a Kingdom. He had a family, and he was learning English. Not that he would ever have a chance to use it in his life, but that is what he liked to do for one reason or another. We cannot say that he was destitute. We have even less grounds to suggest that he was rich, or wealthy. As a matter of fact, he was just trying to keep his body and soul together, hence, he was living in extreme poverty and so was his family. As Russians elegantly put it, he was as poor as a church mouse. The young man was not complaining, not because he was particularly proud, not because he had nobody to confide in, but because nobody cared, and it did not make much sense to complain in such circumstances. Fine, he tried his very best to support his family, but it did not work very well. Poor thing.

And so it came to pass that he discovered that he had a life-string. Do not ask me what it was, I do not know. However, it so happened that this Kingdom needed this life-string badly, this thing was in great demand, it was in deficit and the Kingdom wanted it. THEM started with a trial run, it worked just fine, I mean pulling that life-string from that young man for some unknown purpose. His family became better off and it seemed like a good solution to his problems. Everyone was proud of him, he did not become much wealthier but instead better known and even famous. Newspapers were publishing his photographs, which needed more and more retouching over time.

The product was given the proud name LifeS™. THEM produced a five-year plan, built a factory around that young man, who did not look young any more. THEM did not care. Well, THEM did not in fact care about anything except money.

After a while, everything became a routine—THEM were pulling his LifeS™ from him, so what? He was a hero, he was great, let us give him a State Order, for God's sake. By popular demand, THEM made a special *Order of the First Degree* for him, and were just waiting to hand it to the hero on the next Anniversary of the Great Thing (no-one remembered what it was actually about, but everyone liked to celebrate it).

THEM came to him dressed in beautiful gowns and could hardly find him in the middle of the LifeS™ extraction machine. It was quite expensive to disconnect him, so he was chained permanently to this machine to ensure the five-year plan was implemented. No one could actually remember how long ago he became just a part of the LifeS™ extraction machine, and no one cared. The young man without his LifeS™ turned into an old man and was barely recognisable even to his family, perhaps he had gone insane, perhaps he had acquired the Wisdom, perhaps he was just murmuring something unintelligible to his family, we do not know. But the machine was too noisy, and it was too expensive to stop it. He said what he wanted to say and then died, and the machine was still uselessly working for a while. The LifeS™ was over, and so was his life…

The Kingdom did not notice any change for a while, but very soon it started to crack and deteriorate everywhere. Whatever THEM were using the LifeS™ for, it turned out to be essential for the sheer survival of the Kingdom, so now the Kingdom was breaking into pieces. THEM survived, but THEM have always survived, so far at least. THEM started using special state reserves of LifeS™, THEM found other weaker LifeS™ producers and also lacerated them all to death. As it has always been, and as it is always going to be, THEM did not care diddly-squat. Nothing helped, the situation kept getting worse.

THEM are alive and kicking in the Kingdom of Moscow, 2011. Now THEM do not need Russian people, because THEM are pumping LifeS™ from Russia itself, and the whole country is in a web of gas and oil pipelines. We know already how important LifeS™ is for their survival, so it dictates all the domestic and foreign policy, cultural and social life, religion, and in fact everything in the new Kingdom in general.

This book has given us a unique tool – the magic LifeS™ prism. If you look through this prism, you will see the raison d'être of any event that happened in Russia. A war in the Caucasus in August 2008? Not a problem. We only need to look for critical pipelines, oil-derricks and we will figure out why Russian tanks were in red alert waiting for the barbaric and senseless (from the military tactics point of view) intrusion of Georgia into South Ossetia to happen so that they could instantly occupy the territory of interest. Our LifeS™ prism will focus on the competition between Russia and the USA over the control of oil production and transport in Azerbaijan, and then specifically on the Azerbaijan-Supsa pipeline that passes through South Ossetia.

The LifeS™ prism will reveal the reasons behind the North Stream pipeline, the apartment bombing in Russia before the 2000 presidential election and many other events. I wonder what THEM have in store for the 2012 presidential election. A fresh tranche of apartment bombings? A nice synchronised neo-Nazi riot all over Russia like that in the centre of Moscow in December 2010? Europe frozen to death due to a shortage of natural gas? We will see in due course.

The scale of THEM's appetite for our planet's LifeS™ will depend, of course, on the number and growth rate of THEM. We know that there were about sixty thousand supporters of the RSDRP[141] party in 1907, 102,000 Bolsheviks in 1919[142], approximately 2.4 million Soviet bureaucrats in the mid-1980s[143] and about three million subjects belonging to all strata of the Soviet Nomenklatura (including family members) by the end of the Soviet period[144], which doubled by 2010[145], such that the newly advertised Putin's Peoples' Front in Russia is expected to unite about five million people in the brink of the Presidential election campaign of 2012[146]. Hence, based on 1919-2010 data, the doubling time of THEM has been quite consistent at 15.2 years, which corresponds to an annual growth rate of about 4.6%[147]. This number is slightly below the 6% threshold of the growth rate of cancer cells that is considered aggressive and unfavourably high for the survival of the host[148]. I suppose it makes sense for both of them to keep their growth rate below this threshold to ensure longer survival.

Trajectory and Epilogue

Before publication, I gave a few randomly selected stories from this book to a few people with different educational backgrounds living in different countries to read and comment. Some of the readers were very devoted to their own experiences and pre-existing stereotypes about how, in their mind, things in the Soviet Union used to be, and were reluctant to take a fresh look at this issue. It was also a commonly held view that even if a particular problem may have existed at the time, there was certainly no such problem any longer, that Russia was moving towards democracy etc, etc. Those that had travelled to Russia in the mid-1980s met only nice friends and colleagues, the shops and all the rest of it was just fine. It prompted me to think about this phenomenon.

I realised that the presence of such a category of readers suggests that THEM are in fact very effective at letting Westerners see, hear and even smell exactly what they are supposed to. For example, I remember participating in a discussion forum between Russian and foreign young people in the context of the Moscow Festival of Youth and Students in the summer of 1985. I was trying to make a career for myself at the time, so I would volunteer for various completely senseless Komsomol jobs, such as this one. The Russian side was predominantly made up of people without any knowledge of foreign languages. Surrounded by several identical Russian people, I was trying to communicate with a French student, who just like me knew a bit of German and English. She said this had been their only opportunity to speak to real Russians. Perhaps she still thinks that nearly all Russians look the same, that all have muscles of steel, strong chins and cheekbones, polite faces and unclouded eyes. THEM may have been working on making this a reality ever since the Revolution, but it is not quite true yet.

Let's have a think about the trajectory of events from the Great Socialist October Revolution in 1917 to the demise of the communist party in 1991. Since everything has been always planned, one can surmise that the dissolution of the communist party was part of their plan, too. What was the point? If I knew that, I would be either dead already or President of Russia.

-    *Could you speculate about this a bit more?*
-    THEM *made Russia follow a particular trajectory, which required quite an original set of moral values and human rights associated with the Communist Party. I think that at some point THEM felt that this set became redundant, outdated, or maybe ineffective, so they got rid of it together with the Party. This unexpected move was also meant to disorient the people and make THEM believe that the Soviet regime was over.*

The stories compiled in this book show that by and large, not much has changed since the mid-1980s. The shop shelves might be more full, and there might be a Western perception of freedom and democracy, but the reality is that you can still be detained, beaten and mugged by any policeman (and the number of closed cases are increasing), your property can still be confiscated, your house violated without cause or reason, any foreign or domestic organisation can be closed and pronounced *persona non grata* at any time. THEM are continuing to carry out their eternal noble duty.

Let us put some landmarks on this trajectory starting from the execution of the Russian Tsar Nicolas II together with all his family, doctor and servants in Yekaterinburg on 17 January 1919. We will see on this road the Russian Civil War (twenty million victims), a famine in 1920-1921 (five million), the Cossack genocide (6 million), the first emigration wave in the early 1920s (three and a half to four million), the collectivisation programme with a further famine in 1932-1933 (four to seven and a half million) and the deportation of wealthy peasants, kulaks (~one and a half million families, i.e. about 6 million people), WWII, which some people say was part of their plan for a World Revolution (twenty-one to thirty-one million casualties on the Russian side alone), the second emigration wave in 1940-1950 (eight to ten million), the complete deportation of fourteen ethnic groups and partial deportation of 48 more bad ethnic groups from their traditional territories, crowned with the Gulag forced labour camps in 1921-1953 (four million inmates, 1.4 million of which were executed or died), the third emigration wave in 1960-1980 (one million) and the fourth emigration wave in 1990-2000 (one million).

Altogether, the rule of THEM resulted in the total loss of one hundred and thirty-eight million Russian people. Interestingly, based on the trends of population growth at the beginning of the twentieth century, D. I. Mendeleev[149] estimated that in the year 2000 the population of Russia should reach 594.3 million people (in reality, it was 145.2 million people[150]). Thus, this shortfall by three hundred and eleven million people over the entire twentieth century can be accounted for by the direct loss of one hundred and thirty-eight million people plus a further one hundred and seventy-three million owing to the reduction in the birth rate.

Clearly, THEM must have been dead serious about their trajectory… However, where to does THEM's trajectory lead us all? This question bothers not only me. Georgian film director Tenghiz Abuladze made a cult movie called Repentance (1984), which was a complex theistic allegory about the Stalin era and THEM's trajectory into the future, if you like. The last words of the film were:

Why do we need this way at all if it does not lead us to the temple of God?

THE END

Endnotes

1 **Leonid Ilyich Brezhnev (1906-1982)**, member of the Politburo (1957-1982) of the Central Committee of the communist party of the Soviet Union, the Secretary General of the communist party of the Soviet Union (1964-1982), the highest post in the communist party hierarchy.

2 The footage of a typical parade in 1977 can be watched online at http://etvnet.com/tv/dokumentalnyie-filmyi-online/voennyij-parad-i-demonstratsiya-trudyaschihsya-posvyaschennyie-60-j-godovschine-oktyabrya/205750/ (click on the green PLAY symbol).

3 **Feng Shui,** (literary 'wind water') is part of an ancient Chinese philosophy of nature. This Chinese practice combines the laws of astronomy and geography to help people live productive lives and receive their Qi (energy flow).

4 **G. P. Yakunin** (DOB 4 march 1934), a Russian priest and dissident, member of the Moscow Helsinki group, member of the Russian Parliament 1990-1999, author of the open letter (1965) to the Patriarch of Moscow Alexius I, where he maintained that the Russian Orthodox Church should be liberated from state control including that of the KGB. As a Member of Parliament, he investigated the Soviet coup attempt in 1992 and published the materials supporting the ongoing collaboration between the Moscow Patriarchate and KGB.

5 **'Mathematical' jokes** of the time maintained that in this case 'electricity is Communism minus Soviet power'.

6 **Holy Patriarch Tikhon** (1865-1925), the Holy Patriarch of Moscow and All-Russia in 1918-1925 who proclaimed an anathema on the Bolsheviks and the Soviet regime as an incarnation of the Anti-Christ. Evgenij Tuchkov [the head of the 6th counter-religious department of the KGB (then called OGPU)] used falsified evidence obtained from priests brutally tortured in Solovetsky Camp to prosecute Patriarch Tikhon for the counter-revolutionary plot. Patriarch Tikhon was imprisoned and died allegedly poisoned by the OGPU.

7 **Patriarch Kirill** (Vladimir Gundyaev by passport), allegedly a billionaire and a former KGB operative, made his fortune in tobacco, alcohol, and oil sales. Apparently, the new Patriarch deals on Stock Exchange. He is also fond of car racing, downhill skiing, and breeding exclusive kinds of dogs. He owns villas in Switzerland and conveniently a penthouse with a view of the Cathedral of Christ the Saviour in Moscow. More on his business profile http://www.facebook.com/topic.php?uid=4215648590&topic=7621

8 **Nikita Mikhalkov** (DOB, 21/10/1945), a leading Russian film director, Head of the Russian Cinematographer's Union, winner of the Academy Award for best Foreign Language Film 'Burnt by the sun' ('Утомлённые солнцем', 1994). Full text of the Memorandum http://www.polit.ru/kino/2010/10/26/manifest.html

9 **'Pravda'** ('Правда', 'Truth') was the principal official newspaper of the Soviet Union, an official organ of the Central Committee of the communist party through the entire pre- and Soviet period 1908-1991. Apparently, this newspaper was funded from Germany by the Russian emigrant Alexander Parvus to ensure Bolshevik's victory in 1917. During the Soviet period the circulation rose from 300,000 in July 1917 to 10.6 million in 1975.

10 **Famine 1920-1921** in Russia in Volga region, which spread also to Ukraine and Crimea peninsula. The famine was caused by the excessive food expropriation, civil war and Bolshevik genocide policy. The number of victims is estimated to be 5 million. Another major famine 1932-1933 is thought to have been provoked by NKVD (former KGB) in all Russia, Ukraine, Kazakhstan and Caucasus region with estimated 4-7.5 million victims. See letters of the witnesses at http://www.izvestia.ru/hystory/article3098726/

11 **Dacha (Дача)** a cottage built on state-owned land which was distributed to people usually through work places. It was used by the owners to grow fruit and vegetables during the summer holidays. In winter you could easily identify the dacha owners by

their less grey and slightly swollen "potato faces", as you still can see in the early Van Gogh paintings.

12 **Red Square (Красная площадь)** is located in the heart of Moscow surrounded by the Kremlin, St. Basil's Cathedral, GUM State Department Store and the State Historical Museum. The name of this square is actually translated incorrectly as "red". In fact, the meaning is 'beautiful', just like in old Russian 'red maiden' means 'beautiful girl'. To THEM everything appears to be red, because THEM just do not seem to appreciate this subtlety of the Russian language.

13 **Retired people** would usually have about half of this amount. Pensioners would still need to pay rent and bills (cold water was free), such that they 'preferred' eating only bread, milk and potatoes. Even 25 years after the 1980s, interestingly, Russian pensioners still 'prefer' cheap milk, bread, gruel and grains, if they can afford this, of course.

14 **Geiger counter**, a portable radioactive particle counter that allows to measure ionizing radiation (beta particles and gamma rays).

15 **Fyodor Dostoevsky** (1821-1881), one of the most influential Russian writers and essayists world-renowned for his psychological novels 'Brothers Karamazov' ('Братья Карамазовы') and 'Crime and punishment' ('Преступление и наказание'). He also wrote 'The possessed' ('Бесы') exploring the psychology of THEM, and this novel was banned in the USSR. He wrote in a 'stream of consciousness' literary style to better reproduce spiritual life, experiences and associations. This method was used also by other writers such as James Joyce ('Ulysses'), Publius Ovidius Nason ('Metamorphoses') and Valentin Louis Georges Eugène Marcel Proust ('A la recherché du temps perdu', 'In Search of Lost Time').

Anton Chekhov (1860-1904), Russian short-story writer and physician, world-famous as a playwright with his 'Uncle Vanya' ('Дядя Ваня'), 'Three Sisters' ('Три сестры') and 'The Cherry Orchard' ('Вишнёвый сад') being internationally renowned and actively staged all over the world.

Leo Tolstoy (1828-1910), is considered one of the greatest Russian writers ever. Tolstoy is acclaimed for his major realistic novels 'War and Peace' (the correct translation is 'War and Society', 'Война и мир') and 'Anna Karenina'.

A. S. Pushkin (1799-1837) is considered the best Russian poet ever, the founder of the Russian language, the one who managed to capture the core of the Russian soul, the finest aristocrat and gentleman. His legacy therefore is not just related to poetry, which defined and influenced all subsequent Russian poets, but also to the understanding of the relationship between art, politics and society, the responsibility of the poet etc. Pushkin is also famous for his novels and poems, some of which became librettos for operas. Pushkin's popularity in Russia remains unquestionable and beyond rivalry.

16 **'Ogonyok' magazine** exists since 1899. In the Soviet period, this illustrated conservative magazine targeted Soviet intelligentsia.

17 **Vladimir Nabokov** (1899-1977), Russian-American writer, literary critic, poet, translator, entomologist, known in the Western literature as the author of the novel 'Lolita' (1955). Nabokov's style is characterised by a complex literary technique, deep analysis of the emotional status of the characters, deep interest in the creative thinking underlying the literary process.

18 **Andrei Platonov** (1899-1951), a very interesting and original Soviet writer, whose style and themes were influenced by F. Kafka. Platonov explored the experience of building socialism in Russia from the existentialist positions, as a senseless, brutal and inhuman process.

19 **M. A. Bulgakov (1891-1940),** the author of the novel 'Master and Margarita' (1936). The novel was never published during the author's life. The novel has two intertwining plot lines; one narrates the story of Jesus Christ from his trial to his crucifixion written by a Master, while the other recounts Satan's adventures in Moscow in the early 1920s. At the end, Satan meets Master in a psychiatric clinic to save his soul.

20 **Twelve Chairs** (published in 1928) by I. Ilf and E. Petrov is a satirical novel about the con-artist O. Bender who travels through Russia in the early 1920s looking for a treasure hidden in the base of a chair, allowing us to see the effect of the Revolution on the human perception of reality and changes in the national character. The novel was severely censored and was not really considered anti-Soviet, but was treated with suspicion. It is one of those stories that's funny, but could never have a happy ending.

21 **Maurice Druon** (1918-2009) was a French novelist, member of the Académie Française (1966-2009), Minister of Cultural Affairs (1973-1974). He is best known for a series of seven historical novels under the title 'Les Rois Maudits' ('The Accursed Kings') published in the 1950s.

22 **'Tolkuchka'.** This term could be described as 'a black market of books to wander around with the aim of spotting a book you want, although the books are displayed only for a brief moment as if by chance'.

23 **V. Suvorov** (DOB 20/04/1947), penname of a GRU (Soviet Military Intelligence, 'Государственное Разведовательное Управление') defector living in the UK. His main works are 'Icebreaker: Who started the Second World War?' ('Ледокол', 1990) defending an argument that it was Stalin who was preparing for WWII as a method of propagating communism throughout the world, and that Hitler just pre-empted the first strike of the Soviet Union; and 'Aquarium' (1985) – an autobiography focussed on his training as an GRU officer.

24 http://www.chtenie-21.ru/smi/44

25 http://yfrog.com/h4l2hij

26 **NarKomStat**, is an independent Internet-based non-profit organization, which collects, analyses and publishes real statistics based on data collected from real people (http://www.narkomstat.ru/).

27 The results of the monthly study between 15/10/2010 and 15/11/2010 (http://www.narkomstat.ru/expstats/).

28 http://www.promurman.ru/articles/23-04-2009.shtml?&print=1

29 http://www.tula-oblast.ru/news229

30 **Pyrrhic victory** refers to the defeat of Roman army at Heraclea in 280 BC, after which the winning party King Pyrrhus of Epirus said: "Another such victory and I come back to Epirus alone".

31 **The 'Gulag Archipelago' (1968) by A. Solzhenitsyn** explored the communist repressive genocide system based on slavery exploitation of prisoners and indeed all Russian people as the main drive of economic development of the communist state, between 1918-1956. Gulag stands for 'Head Office LAGerey (concentration camps)', which belonged to NKVD (former KGB). Solzhenitsyn's study is based on archives, collection of personal memoirs of Gulag prisoners and witnesses, as well as on the author's personal Gulag experience. This book was considered as the top anti-Soviet propaganda work; reading and distributing the book was a serious criminal offence and was treated as such with the 'mercilessness of the triumphant proletariat'. For example, in 1973 one of Solzhenitsyn's secretaries E. Voronyanskaya was subjected to KGB interrogation and revealed the whereabouts of one copy of this book. She was released and committed suicide on the same day. I happen to know from a documentary that KGB interrogation techniques include hitting women's genitalia, which is a strong argument.

32 **S. Belkowski**, a political analyst and communication specialist, founder and director of the National Strategy Institute and the communication company PolyTech.

33 **Gazprom**, the biggest natural gas exploring, producing and distributing company and the largest business in Russia. In 2008 the company produced 549.7 billion cubic meters of natural gas (seventeen% of the world production); Revenue: 99.1 billion US dollars (2009), net income: 25.7 billion US dollars.

34 **SurgutNefteGas**, one of the largest Russian oil and gas producing companies. Revenue: 18.8 billion US dollars; net income: 2.9 billion US dollars.

35 **GunVor International BV**, is the third largest energy trading company in the world. Revenue: 90 billion US dollars; net income: 70 billion US dollars (2008) (http://navalny.livejournal.com/241270.html?thread=3473270). (Interestingly, 'vor' means 'thief' in Russian).

36 **Yukos** (1993-2007), was one of the most successful oil companies in Russia in 2000-2003 controlled by a Russian businessman **Mr. Mikhail Khodorkovsky**. On a case of tax evasion, Mr. Khodorkovsky was sentenced to 8 years in prison, the company seized to exist, and all former business is currently channelled via GunVor International BV (http://www.novayagazeta.ru/data/2008/80/07.html). Mr. Khodorkovsky was tried again 22 October 2010 and received another fourteen years for stealing 200 million tons of oil (http://khodorkovsky.ru/). 'Quod licet Iovi, non licet bovi' ('What is legitimate for Jupiter, is not legitimate for oxen').

37 **'Das Kapital' (The Capital)** (1867) is a theoretical treatise on economics by Karl Heinrich Marx (1818-1883) in which he analysed the capitalist process of production. 'The communist Manifesto' (1848) is a classical communist document, which formulated the main dogmas of this philosophy. It considers human history as a history of 'class struggle', and that capitalism would be replaced by communism through the "dictatorship of the proletariat", which Marx considered as the most advanced class in society.

38 **Special elite language schools** offering intensive foreign language (French, German and English) tuition appeared in Moscow from 1963. There was a strong rumour going around in the early 1990s that the language course programme was endorsed by the KGB and was aimed at the acquisition of interpretation and translation skills, rather than colloquial skills, by the pupils.

39 **Cuban missile crisis** (14 October - 14 November 1962). A military confrontation between the Soviet Union and the USA over the deployment of Soviet nuclear missiles in Cuba, which nearly caused the last nuclear war. It was, of course, a political and not linguistic crisis.

40 **In 1985-1986**, there were 82 special elite language schools in Moscow (http://www.nir.ru/Socio/scipubl/sj/sj99-chered.html).

41 http://teach-learn.narod.ru/school.htm

42 **Little Octobrist** was a political youth organisation for children seven to nine years of age preparing them to become a **Young Pioneer**, which was a similar organisation for children of ten to fifteen years of age. Then the young person aged between fifteen to twenty-eight years would be taken over by **Komsomol,** and if he/she wanted to become one of THEM, then there were limited possibilities to become a member of the communist party of the Soviet Union. Contrary to common beliefs, only a fraction of people were members of the communist party (about nineteen million party members in 1986, or ten percent population of the USSR) and those were primarily recruited from the working class and military. There were strict quotas for all other people.

43 **Karl Kautsky** (1854-1938) was an economist, historian, the Founder and the Leader of the Second International (Bolshevik fraction of the Russian Social Democratic party), one of the leaders of German Social Democracy. Lenin incorrectly criticised him for being a renegade who betrayed his own views.

44 **Clara Zetkin** (1857-1933) was one of the leaders of German Social Democracy.

45 **PhD minima**. A doctoral student needed to pass 3 exams called PhD minima: in a chosen professional field say, mineralogy, in a foreign language and in 'scientific communism'.

46 Lenin's older brother, Alexander Ulyanov, participated in an assassination attempt on the Russian tsar Alexander III, was sentenced to death and executed May 1887. A popular belief holds that Lenin's activity was aiming at taking revenge for his brother.

47 **Apostle Paul** (c. 5 – c. 67) commented on the Civil Obedience in 'Epistle to the Romans' (13:1-7) '**1**. Let every person be subject to the governing authorities. For there is no authority except by

God's appointment and the authorities that exist have been instituted by God. **2.** So the person who resists such authority resists the ordinance of God, and those who resist will incur judgment...' The St. Paul's doctrine does not consider the possibility that the government could be instituted by Satan (http://www.reformedtheology.ca/romans13.html).

48 **Soviet Republics**. The Soviet Union (or in full, the Union of Soviet Socialist Republics, or USSR) as a federation, consisted of fifteen Soviet Republics which had a certain degree of independence in the form of the national language, flag, coat of arms and anthem. Otherwise the structure of the organs of power was similar, with the communist party having the pivotal role of in all aspects of life.

49 **Diogenes of Sinope** (412-323 BC) – a Greek philosopher-cynic who allegedly lived in Athens in a barrel in extreme poverty as a protest against social values and institutions.

50 **Mycobacterium tuberculosis** (Koch's Bacillus), the bug that causes tuberculosis, a life-threatening infectious disease affecting the lungs, some internal organs and sometimes joints, characterised by high mortality. According to the Institute Pasteur, Paris, France, this bug is likely to have first appeared on Earth as early as 3 million years ago, such that this malady is likely to be one of the oldest human infectious diseases. Tuberculosis morbidity is associated with poor health services, poverty, hunger and therefore is considered a 'social' disease, for the eradication of which vaccination, specific treatment and improvement of living conditions are necessary.

51 **Felix Dzershinsky** (1877-1926), a distinguished Bolshevik of Polish origin who created the first Soviet Secret Service called 'Cheka' ('Чрезвычайная комиссия', 'Extraordinary Commission', i.e. commission with extraordinary rights) on 20 December 1917. The main mission of the Cheka was to combat counterrevolution and deal with sabotage, but it was also responsible for the organisation of the first Gulag labour camps, requisition of food and

suppression of the rebellions of peasants, as well as with restraining the desertions from the Red Army.

52 **Maxim Gorky** (1868-1936), a pseudonym of Alexei Maximovitch Peshkov who was a prominent proletarian writer and a political advocate of the Marxist ideology and the Soviet regime. Gorky is considered the founder of the new literary direction of socialist realism, which postulated that literature should depict life not as it is but as it was supposed to be. In this precise vein, Gorky wrote many propaganda works that supported Stalin's genocide, Gulag labour camps and other atrocities of the Soviet regime. He and his son were allegedly assassinated on Stalin's direct order on 18 June 1936 (http://trst.narod.ru/orlov/xxii.htm).

53 **Pinocchio**, is the main imaginary character of 'The Adventures of Pinocchio' (1883) by Carlo Collodi. This wooden puppet went through many adventures to solve the mystery of the golden key that unlocked a secret door into a magic world. Pinocchio did this by accident when he punctured a hole in the picture of a family hearth with his wooden nose and found the cherished door.

54 http://www.rg.ru/2010/05/20/kvartira.html

55 **Mr. Bulanov** is a former Prefect of the Moscow South Region (area ~131 km^2, i.e. 12.2% of Moscow). His collection of properties and declared income are typical for this rank in the hierarchy of Moscow Housing Authorities (http://www.vesti.ru/doc.html?id=400978).

56 **Yin and Yang**, similar to the philosophical law of unity and struggle of opposites, the Chinese Yin and Yang represent the core principle of the Chinese philosophy where Yin is the positive (masculine) side of the Universe, and Yang – the negative (feminine). Both Yin and Yang exist as a unity in a constant struggle, but one cannot be without another.

57 The South Administrative region of Moscow is full of promising acquisition objects ranging from the largest in Moscow car plant SIL to state heritage parks and architectural complexes, such as Tsaritsyno or Kolomenskoje (http://www.prime-realty.ru/cmi/c2/2.158..htm).

58 **Mr. Alpatov** is current Prefect of the Western Moscow region (http://www.rian.ru/economy/20100504/230368432.html).

59 http://www.newsru.com/world/23jun2006/matvienka.html

60 http://www.newsru.com/russia/05jun2006/island.html

61 **'Moskovskaya Vodka'** is considered the best Russian vodka. All technology and underlying vodka research was carried out in Moscow. In the 1980s it was sold in 0.5 litre bottles, which did not match the traditional Russian measurements of vodka. Traditionally vodka was sold in subdivisions of a 'Moscow bucket' (twelve litres), such as a quarter (3 litres) called 'Chetvert' ('четверть'), a tenth (1.2 litres) called 'Stoff' ('штоф'), a fifteenth (0.8 litres) called 'Kruzhka' ('кружка'), a twentieth (0.6 litres) called 'Butil' ('бутыль'), with the smallest flask equivalent of a fortieth of a bucket known as 'Krasovul'' ('красовул') being 0.3 litres. The optimal intake of vodka is about 0.2 litres, such that one 'Butil' should be optimal for 3 people, whereas 0.5 litre bottles are too small for three and too large for two people.

62 **First alcoholic drinks** similar to vodka appeared in Russia as early as 950-1100 AD; however the production of vodka as we know it today in Russia was proven to be established between 1448 and 1478. However, the first written formal usage of the word 'vodka' in an official Russian document could be found only in the decree of Empress Elizabeth of 8 June 1751 because this term was used primarily to refer to medicines and tinctures rather than to an alcoholic drink.

63 **'Pelmeni'** ('Пельмени'), a traditional Russian (Siberian) dumpling dish made with a meat filling wrapped in a thin pastry. In Siberia, pelmeni are made in galactic numbers, frozen outside and then stored frozen until use. After boiling them with salt and onion, pelmeni would be served usually with meat broth, crème fraîche, vinegar or butter. 'Vodochka' is one of the best accompaniments to this 'music of the heart', linking the pure enjoyment of the body with the nirvana of the soul.

64 **'Aqua vitae'** (Latin: 'water of life') is an aqueous solution of ethanol which was distilled and prepared in the Middle Ages in monasteries.

65 **An ideal initial sequence** for drinking 'vodochka', according to our several centuries' experience, would be to drink a 50 ml double-shot 'glassie' with minimal food (a 'breadie' with 'herringie' would suffice), wait for a few minutes and then have another 'glassie' with more food after that. This sequence would allow you to reach the most pleasant status of being slightly tipsy, which should persist even without drinking for a relatively long time.

66 **Byzantine Empire** (IV-XIII centuries AD), an orthodox Greek-speaking part of the Roman Empire which existed in the Middle Ages with the capital city of Constantinople. The decline of this Empire is thought to be associated with the treason of the ruling part of society who had given up the Orthodox faith, traditional moral and cultural values, and their national identity due to their own political interests and disbelief in their own people.

67 Data   from   September   2009   (http://en.rian.ru/russia/20090924/156238102.html).

68   http://www.intelros.ru/readroom/foma/f_03_2008/1980-pjanstvo-v-rossii-tolko-fakty.html

69 http://otvet.mail.ru/question/25654383/

70 http://www.pravoslavie.ru/smi/1233.htm

71 http://www.narodsobor.ru/default.asp?trID=392&artID=3364

72 http://www.vz.ru/news/2010/1/22/368865.html

73 http://www.fms.gov.ru/press/publications/news_detail.php?ID=11276

74 http://www.narodsobor.ru/default.asp?trID=392&artID=3364

75 http://www.rpnp.ru/pnp/hotnews/hot_news_024.htm

76 **Zbigniew Brzezinski** was President Carter's national security adviser in 1977-81. Currently, Mr. Brzezinski is an Adjunct Professor of American Foreign Policy at Johns Hopkins University's Nitze School of Advanced International Studies and Counsellor to the Centre for Strategic and International Studies in Washington, D.C.

77 http://revolutionarypolitics.com/?p=2717

78 **Vasily Perov** (1833-1882) painted the 'Tea party in Mytishchi near Moscow' (1862) with a single priest drinking tea and other people around him serving, begging or doing chores.

79 **Ivan Kulikov** (1875-1941) is famous for his painting 'Tea party in a peasant hut' (1902), for which he was awarded a Gold medal, the title of an artist and the right to go abroad. The picture shows the traditional Russian folk tea ceremony with people wearing their best garments and drinking tea out of a saucer.

80 **Boris Kustodiev** (1878-1927) painted 'The merchant's wife at tea' (1918), which shows the necessary attributes of the tea drinking procedure, such as a samovar to keep the water hot, as well as the accompanying fruit, cakes and jams.

81 **Tea drinking** was particularly popular in Moscow, with the main tea businesses operating from the city and selling tea to other parts of Russia. As a result, Muscovites are sometimes still called in other parts of Russia 'водохлёбы' ('water-drinkers').

82 **The facts about tea** used in this story are taken from a unique monograph 'Tea' by William Vasiljevich Pokhlebkin. Highly recommended for those who enjoy drinking tea, and to learn how to make it properly.

83 **Tea prices in Russia** at the beginning of the 20th century were about ten times higher than in England.

84 **Tea production in the Soviet Union** started from late 1940s and by the mid-1980s it was well-established in three main regions: Georgia, Azerbaijan and Krasnodar with the best teas called the 'Bouquet of Georgia', 'Bouquet of Azerbaijan' and 'Krasnodar's

Bouquet'. The production of black tea in Russia was discontinued by the early 1990s, which coincided with the dissolution of the Soviet Union. Whether the deficit of high-quality tea was a cause or consequence of this political event, is not known.

85 **Russian sauna** or banya was first mentioned allegedly in 1113 in the Russian Primary Chronicle, where the life and work of the missionary Apostle St. Andrew is described. More on the history and banya tradition at http://cyberbohemia.com/Pages/russianbaniahistory.htm

86 **Russian-English translation** from the first stanza of 'Internationale' communist anthem originally written by Eugène Pottier in 1871. This line in the original French-English translation is much milder 'Le monde va changer de base' (The world is about to change its foundation). There was no original plan to destroy the foundations of the world; this was a subsequent addition to the apocalypic scenario.

87 **Smolny Institute of Noble Maidens, St. Petersburg, Russia** was founded by Russian Empress Catherine II in 1764. The building was commissioned by the Society for Education of Noble Maidens and constructed in 1806-1808. The building was chosen by Vladimir Ilyich Lenin as the Bolshevik headquarters during the October Revolution in 1917. After moving the national government to Moscow in 1918, the Smolny became the headquarters of the local communist party apparatus.

88 **D. S. Merezhkovsky** (1985-1941), a Russian poet and writer, author of the trilogy 'Christ and Anti-Christ' (1895-1905) and 'The Kingdom of the Beast' (1908-1918) – an intellectual historical-philosophical contemplation on the history of mankind from the viewpoint of the struggle between Christ and the Anti-Christ.

89 **Leonid Ilyich Brezhnev** had been awarded 114 Soviet Orders and medals during his life, including the highest Soviet awards, such as 4 Orders of the Hero of the Soviet Union (the highest Order of the Soviet Union, which was usually given to heroes for sacrificing their lives), 8 Orders of Lenin, 2 Orders of the October Revolution, 2

Orders of the Red Flag, as well as the Order of Victory. He also held awards from the Soviet bloc countries, such that the total number, according to some estimates, was in excess of 200.

90 **Leonid Brezhnev** 'wrote' three books: 'Malaya Zemlya' ('Малая земля', 'Small land'), 'Vozroshdeniye' ('Возрождение', 'Renaissance') and 'Tselina' ('Целина', 'Virgin land'), which in fact were written by a group of professional journalists Arkady Sahnin, Anatoly Agranovsky and Alexander Murzin, respectively. These books were made part of the school curriculum, obligatory discussions and lectures, TV talk shows, such that about fifteen million copies were sold altogether and 179,241 roubles (>8 years' average salary) royalties paid to the most published author in the Soviet Union of all time – Leonid Ilyich Brezhnev. For those interested, Leonid Brezhnev also left his memoirs written by another group of journalists, where he assumed the honourable responsibility for the WWII victory and the highly successful Soviet space programme of the 1960s-1970s.

91 **On 16 October 1941,** the Central Committee of the communist party of the Soviet Union decided to evacuate the government, Soviet organisation and power structures from Moscow due to the serious military situation, with German troops positioned as close as 30 kilometres from the Kremlin. By late October – early November 1941 Moscow turned into a ghost city and was dominated by looting and other criminal activity. Muscovites felt abandoned by their government.

92 **Yuri Vladimirovich Andropov** (1914-1984), member of the Politburo of the Central Committee of the communist party of the Soviet Union (1973-1984), the Secretary-General of the Central Committee of the CPSU (1982-1984), the Chief of the KGB (1967-1982). Andropov was one of the three main KGB gurus, as he transformed the KGB into the best secret service in the world. The two others were Felix Dzerzhinsky, who created the KGB (then Cheka, 20 December 1917), and Heinrich Müller (Chief of the Gestapo – the Secret State Police in Nazi Germany), who developed the best counter-intelligence service in 1941-1945.

93 **Constantin Ustinovich Chernenko** (1911-1985), member of the Politburo (1978-1985), then Secretary-General of the Central Committee of the CPSU (13 February 1984-10 March 1985).

94 http://www.vesti.ru/doc.html?id=400978

95 http://www.internovosti.ru/text/?id=28148

96 **Soviet Nomenklatura**. Stalin defined the requirements for nomenklatura as 'people who can carry out directives - who are able understand the directive, to accept it as their own thought and to implement it.' The Soviet Nomenklatura was based mainly on the communist party structures, and its training included a rotation system to include work in industry, in Soviet and party organs. The highest Nomenklatura stratum was occupied by the members of the Central Committee of the CPSU, which consisted of 22,500 people in 1980.

97 http://www.rb.ru/inform/111427.html

According to the leader of the political party LDPR (Liberal Democratic party of Russia), Mr. V. Zhirinovsky 98 (http://poedinok.net/vladimir-zhirinovskij-i-genri-reznik/).

99 **The acronym 'MIMO'** also has a meaning in Russian as a separate word, 'мимо', meaning to 'pass by', 'miss', 'beside the mark', as if to warn applicants that they were likely to fail the entrance exams.

100 **The communist revolt on board the 'Ochakov' cruiser** under the command of Lieutenant P.P. Schmidt in 1905 during the First Russian Revolution. This cruiser raised a red flag as a sign of rebellion calling on other ships of the Sevastopol fleet to follow suit. The uprising was suppressed by troops loyal to the Tsarist regime, the Cossacks and the gendarmes.

101 **Shipka Pass** is a key connection between Southern and Northern Bulgaria. The Shipka Pass battle took place during the liberation of Bulgaria in the war between Russia and Turkey in 1877-1878.

102 **The State Academic Opera and Ballet Bolshoi Theatre of Russia or just Bolshoi ('Big') Theatre** was founded in 1776 by Royal will of Russian Empress Catherine II. The Bolshoi Theatre is the world renowned centre of classical Russian ballet. The repertoire is focused on classical operas and ballets.

103 **The Beryozka chain of shops** was opened in 1964 to supply foreigners and the Soviet elite with deficit goods, electronics, garments, foodstuffs that were not available in other shops. These shops belonged to VneshPosilTorg and accepted only foreign currency and special vouchers denominated in roubles. Part of the salaries at the top pyramid job level was paid in those vouchers, enabling easy access to highly rare and desirable products. The chain ceased to exist in the early 1990s when the rouble became a hard currency and could be exchanged on the open market.

104 **Kolkhoz (collective farming community)** combined people against their will to share land, resources and labour in the context of large agricultural communities to receive payment in the form of agricultural products and money. Kolkhoz communities started to appear in 1929 after the XV communist party Congress that announced the collectivisation agricultural programme. Before 1929, wealthy farm owners (Kulak) constituted about 3% of the agricultural population and possessed about 33% of machinery and resources. They clearly were against collectivisation and were therefore 'exterminated as a class' (I. V. Stalin). Others were enslaved in 1932 when peasants were deprived of their right to have a passport, which was the only acceptable means of personal identification. This was done to ban any migration from villages and Kolkhoz communities.

105 **Arcady Raikin (1911-1987)** was a famous and highly respected Soviet comedian, film director, scriptwriter and intellectual who all his life fought against THEM in a very subtle way showing how absurd the situation was in the USSR. The monologue above emphasises the absurdness and abnormality of the situation. THEM clearly overlooked this. If there was someone who was actually saying at that time – Folks, this isn't normal... –

then Raikin was the one! The extract refers to the fact that ordinary engineers and footwear department managers were from opposite social strata, like peasants and aristocrats, and that usually they did not mix socially.

106 Federal issue No. 4042 of 13 April 2006 (http://www.rg.ru/2006/04/13/chinovnika.html)

107 **Abridged record** of 'Meeting of President Medvedev with the winners of school and student contests', 18/03/2010; "...science and pedagogy are a vocation... and if a person wants to make money, let us be honest with each other, he should not go into science". (http://kremlin.ru/news/7139). In other words, if you feel that your life's mission is to be a scientist or a teacher, it is very good because we do not need to pay you and stick to the system when 'in the 70s and 80s a very good scientist (Mr. Medvedev was referring to his father) would earn less than a porter'. The gloomy faces of his listeners did not suggest that the young generation is very keen to go into science...

108 **Non-military related losses** in the Russian army according to the official statistics of the Ministry of Defence were 37 (20 suicide cases) for April 2009 (http://www.lenta.ru/news/2009/05/22/losses1/), and 131 for the entire of 2009 (http://forum-msk.org/material/news/1367131.html).

109 http://forum.zakonia.ru/showthread.php?t=100069

110 '**Russia, Shift to the Shadows**', Charles Clover, Financial Times, 16/12/09 (http://www.ocnus.net/artman2/publish/Dark_Side_4/Russia-Shift-to-the-Shadows_printer.shtm).

111 '**The Labour book**' ('Трудовая книжка') was introduced in the Soviet Union in 1939 to record the entire working life of an individual including places of work, positions held, any awards and reprimands received. To this day, it remains the primary document that contains all information required to apply for a state pension.

112 **Magadan** is a Russian port on the Sea of Okhotsk and a gateway to the Kolyma region – the most notorious region for the

Gulag labour camps. The area is rich in gold and platinum and is located within the Arctic Circle with winter temperatures around -40°C and below.

113 'Sputnik-1' was the first satellite in the world launched by the Soviet Union into geocentric orbit on 4 October 1957.

114 'To catch up with and overtake America' was at some point a serious goal of the communist party during Khrushchev's rule, which he formulated at the Central Committee meeting on 22 May 1957. This slogan was applied particularly vigorously in agriculture, and, in essence, it served as an economic indicator of approaching communism, which was supposed to be built in the Soviet Union by 1980. What they seem to have overlooked is that by this indicator, the USA was already living in communism!

115 Thomson Reuters of 26.01.2010 at http://www.alertnet.org/ thenews/newsdesk/N25198050.htm

116 Louis Pasteur (1822-1895), a French chemist and microbiologist who created the first vaccine against rabies and anthrax.

117 In October-mid-November 2010, a total of 46 journalists (one every day, according to the data of Mr. Gusev, the Editor-in-Chief and owner of newspaper 'Moskovskij Komsomolez', talk show 'Poedinok' of 11 November 2010, video footage at http://poedinok.net/pavel-gusev-i-olga-kostina/) were demonstratively and ritually beaten [usually in front of CCTV cameras using metal rods smashing or cutting off victim's fingers and arms (to prevent writing), legs and toes (to prevent walking), jaws (to stop talking) and pelvis (for obvious reasons)]. Most cases were closed, investigations were not carried out. The most characteristic examples include assaults on Mr. Kashin (Moscow, Mr. Kashin was in coma for six days, http://vsoloviev.livejournal.com/309093.html); Mr. Mikhailov (city of Saratov, Mr. Mikhailov is currently in hospital, http://txt.newsru.com/russia/09nov2010/kashin_3.html); Mr. Fetisov (Moscow region) and Mr. Lobanov (city of Perm, the case was closed due to the participation of the son of a militia man in the crime) (http://txt.newsru.com/russia/09nov2010/kashin_3.html)

118 **Current examples of this new trend** include the beatings of Mr. Adamchuk (Moscow region, Mr. Adamchuk was accused of faking his beating, http://www.izvestia.ru/news/news256484) and Mr. Beketov (Moscow region, Mr. Beketov cannot speak and walk after the assault, he was accused of defamation and sentenced to pay a fine, http://www.uralpolit.ru/77/moscow/kriminal/ id_206916.html).

119 **Mikhail Zhvanetsky** (DOB, 06/03/1934), a famous Russian stand-up comedian and satirical writer.

120 http://www.cirota.ru/forum/view.php?subj=81916

121 http://wday.ru/wdaily/obshhestvo/_article/novaya-volna-jemigraczii-iz-rossii-sopostavima-s1/

122 **Dr. Geim and Dr. Novoselov**, two laureates for the Nobel Prize in Physics in 2010 'for ground breaking experiments regarding the two-dimensional material graphene' (http://nobelprize.org/nobel_prizes/physics/laureates/2010/).   Dr. Geim was born in Sochi, Russia, and Dr. Novoselov in Nishniy Tagil, Russia. Both laureates worked at the Institute of Solid State Physics, Chernogolovka, Russia, and are currently at the School of Physics and Astronomy, Manchester University, United Kingdom.

123 http://www.lib.com.ua/books/6/394n17.html

124 **According to this document**, members or candidates for membership of the Politburo of the Central Committee have signed for the following funds transfers (in USD million): N. Slyunkov – 22.15, G. Romanov – 33.0, V. Chebrikov – 38.5, L. Zaikov - 43.0, M. Solomentsev – 53.2, E. Ligachev – 60.6, N. Ryzhkov – 61.2, V. Vorotonikov – 77.2, Yuri Maslyukov - 22.0, V. Kryuchkov – 22.0, V. Medvedev – 22.0, V. Nikonov – 1.2, M. Gorbachev – 117.4, G. Voronov – 117.1, A. Shelepin – 97.0. See more at http://www.nasledie.ru/vibor/article.php?art=19

125 Using the current price of gold at US$28,352 per kilo, 3750 tonnes of gold are worth approximately 106 billion dollars (http://www.duel.ru/200219/?18_3_2).

126 http://enbv.narod.ru/text/Econom/avdokushin-meo/str/p20.html

127 http://www.rg.ru/2011/04/05/ottok-anons.html

128 http://www.rbcdaily.ru/2010/04/06/focus/469241

129 **Cossacks** had established their national identity in Russia (Ryazan region, Siberia, Dnepr River and other parts of Russia) from 1444 and in the Ukraine from 1517. This new group of people consisted initially mainly of fugitives who had fled from the Tatar-Mongol and Lithuanian rule and went into hiding on the many islands of the Dnepr river and formed there a Christian Republic. The key characteristics of the Cossacks have always been great patriotism, military-style organisation of their life and culture, commitment to freedom, to the Orthodox religion and the Russian Empire. This information is taken from 'History of the Russian State' (first published in 1816-1829) (volume 5, chapter 4) by Nikolai Karamzin (1766-1826).

130 **'Red Wheel'** – is a novel by Russian writer, a Nobel laureate in literature A. Solzhenitsyn on the history of Russia from August 1914 to December 1917 covering WWI, February 1917 (Bourgeoisie) and October 1917 (Socialist) Revolutions.

131 **The genocide of the Cossacks** was implemented according to several directives of the communist party (the most prominent being those of 24 January 1919, 3 February 1919 and 8 April 1919). The first directive advised to '… implement terror against wealthy Cossacks with extermination of every one of THEM; implement terror against all Cossacks in general who directly or indirectly took part in the opposition to the Soviet regime. All relevant measures should be applied to the last category of Cossacks to prevent THEM from repeated action against Soviet supremacy'. The second directive demanded 'the physical extermination of at least 100,000 Cossacks aged between eighteen and fifty'. The third directive expressed the core attitude of the Bolsheviks to the Cossacks in that 'the current task is the total, rapid and decisive extermination of Cossacks as a separate economic group of people, including the destruction of their traditional way of life, the physical extermination of the Cossack

officers, Atamans [a title of Cossacks leaders of various calibres] and administrators, the dispersal and neutralisation of all other common Cossacks'. As a result, nearly 35% of the Cossack population from the river Don were killed, with the total number of victims approaching one million (out of about 6 million Cossacks who lived in Russia in 1917). The Cossacks were killed mainly by non-Russian troops, such as those of Chinese, Hungarian and Lithuanian origin, by 'revolutionary sailors' and militants from Caucasus. The complete text of the directives and the consequences can be found at:

http://apologetika.com/modules.php?op=modload&name=News&f ile=article&sid=1106&mode=thread&order=0&thold=0

132 **The State Duma** is the lower house of the Federal Assembly of Russia, whereas the upper house is called The Federation Council of Russia.

133 The situation was discussed on the talk show 'Poedinok' ('Sparring') on 18 November 2010; http://poedinok.net/vladimir-zhirinovskij-i-genri-reznik/). It looks like the Lenin's directive of Cossack extermination is still in force.

134 http://www.skfo.ru/news/2011/02/19/Kazaki_Rossii_ lishayutsya_svoey_demokratii/

135 In the mid-1980s, the Soviet government upgraded the state food distribution policy by introducing 'food orders' or 'food hampers' usually distributed via canteens at work. One of the clear advantages was that ordinary people would spend less time looking for food during their lunch breaks.

136 **Gorbachev's 'dry law'** ('сухой закон'), 1985-1987, was similar to prohibition law (the Noble Experiment) in the USA, 1920-1933. This law envisaged increase in the price of vodka, a restriction of sale times, a reduction in the production of wine, vodka and beer, which led to the eradication of about 30% of all vineyards (http://www.opel-club.com.ua/forum/lofiversion/index.php/t88593.html), wineries and the loss of professional wine-growing expertise in Russia. On the positive side, the anti-alcoholic campaign resulted in some reduction

in alcoholism, but also led to economic losses estimated at one hundred billion roubles (143 billion USD in 1985 money, http://www.opoccuu.com/kurs.htm).

137 **Neznaika** (Незнайка, 'Ignoramus'), a character in the famous Russian fantasy novel trilogy by N. Nosov, where in 'Neznaika in the solar city' ('Незнайка в солнечном городе', 1958) he was known for being so lazy that he slept in his day clothes. The two other novels are entitled 'The adventures of Neznaika and his friends' (1953-1954) and 'Neznaika on the moon' (1964-1965).

138 **one hundred grams of vodka** was first introduced into the military daily ration in the Soviet Army in 1943 after the Battle of Stalingrad (21 August 1942 – 2 February 1943).

139 **Tsetse fly,** an African poisonous fly that transmits a parasite disease called trypanosomiases, which is accompanied with abnormal sleepiness (sleeping sickness).

140 You cannot imagine the smell and sound of this abbreviation, because it was on the other side of the wall. At some point in my life, I had seriously thought that all those places, such as the USA, Germany and so on just did not exist, that they were a product of propaganda, an invention of the competent organs, a dream of all dreams, a fairy tale, another planet, or rather universe, altogether.

141 **RSDRP party** ('Russian Social Democratic Labour party'; 'Русская Социал-Демократическая Рабочая партия'; 1898-1917). After the 1917 October Revolution, the RSDRP was renamed the 'Russian communist party (of Bolsheviks)'; 'Российская Коммунистическая партия (большевиков)') (http://works.tarefer.ru/33/101120/index.html)

142 http://www.pravda-nn.ru/archive/number:452/article:6803/

143 http://ria-stk.ru/mi/adetail.php?ID=45036

144 **Soviet Nomenklatura** from Latin 'Nomenclature' ('list of names', defined as THEM in this book) consisted of people who held principal positions in the communist party, Komsomol, Soviet

and Trade Union organisations, as well as in industry, agriculture, education, science and politics http://www.belousenko.com/ books/publicism/voslensky_nomenklatura.htm

145 http://svpressa.ru/economy/article/30265/

146 http://www.newsland.ru/news/detail/id/698673/cat/94/

147 Population growth rate was calculated using exponential growth and the rule of 70 formula (http://www.ecofuture.org/ pop/facts/exponential70.html).

148 http://www.breastcancer.org/symptoms/diagnosis/rate_grade.jsp)

149 Dmitri Mendeleev (1834-1907), Russian chemist who discovered the Periodic Table of chemical elements (1869). At the end of the 19th century, he predicted the population of the USA to be about 180 million people by the mid-20th century (in reality, it was 179 million in 1959). More on demographic predictions of Mendeleev at http://news.km.ru/rossiya_ne_realizovala_prognoz_m?page=3

150 http://demoscope.ru/weekly/knigi/ns_r00/razdel1g1_1.html

www.ingramcontent.com/pod-product-compliance
Lightning Source LLC
Chambersburg PA
CBHW031510270326
41930CB00006B/338